T0030463

TRANS SEX

of related interest

Queer Sex
A Trans and Non-Binary Guide to Intimacy, Pleasure and Relationships
Juno Roche
ISBN 978 1 78592 406 4
eISBN 978 1 78450 770 1

Top to Bottom
A Memoir and Personal Guide Through Phalloplasty
Finlay Games
ISBN 978 1 78775 587 1
eISBN 978 1 78775 588 8

Trans Power
Own Your Gender
Juno Roche
ISBN 978 1 78775 019 7
eISBN 978 1 78775 020 3

Written on the Body
Letters from Trans and Non-Binary Survivors of
Sexual Assault and Domestic Violence
Edited by Lexie Bean
Foreword and additional pieces by Dean Spade, Nyala Moon,
Alex Valdes, Sawyer DeVuyst and Ieshai Bailey
ISBN 978 1 78592 797 3
eISBN 978 1 78450 803 6

TRANS SEX

SEX

A Guide for Adults

Kelvin Sparks

Jessica Kingsley Publishers
London and Philadelphia

First published in Great Britain in 2023 by Jessica Kingsley Publishers
An imprint of Hodder & Stoughton Ltd
An Hachette Company

1

The information contained in this book is not intended to replace the
services of trained medical professionals or to be a substitute for medical
advice. You are advised to consult a doctor on any matters relating to your
health, and in particular on any matters that may require diagnosis or
medical attention.

A CIP catalogue record for this title is available from the British Library
and the Library of Congress

ISBN 978 1 83997 043 6
eISBN 978 1 83997 044 3

Jessica Kingsley Publishers' policy is to use papers that are natural,
renewable and recyclable products and made from wood grown in
sustainable forests. The logging and manufacturing processes are expected
to conform to the environmental regulations of the country of origin.

Jessica Kingsley Publishers
Carmelite House
50 Victoria Embankment
London EC4Y 0DZ

www.jkp.com

MIX
Paper from
responsible sources
FSC® C013056

This book is dedicated to my partner
and friends, as thanks for all the pots of
coffee, companionship and study/research
sessions they shared with me during the
process of writing. I cannot thank all
of you enough, and this book would
not exist without your help.

Disclaimer

Before you get stuck into reading this trans sex guide, I want to add a disclaimer. This book is not a 'complete' guide to sex as a trans person, nor do I want it to be taken as one. No 'complete' guide to sex can ever be written, let alone for a demographic of people with such varied experiences, bodies and ways of moving through the world. Plenty of the information in this book may not be relevant to your identity, body or way of moving through the world. While I've tried to keep all language as neutral as possible in terms of assigning identities to body parts, medical procedures and ways of moving through the world, I still may use language for bodies and identities that you don't use yourself. If that's the case, I welcome you to edit the language for the language you prefer, take whatever pieces of information you find useful or relevant to your life and way of being, and leave what doesn't suit you or isn't relevant. I ask in return that you are mindful about the other people to whom these parts are valuable.

If there is a part of you and your relationship to sex as a trans person you find isn't reflected in this book, that is due to the book's own limitations and/or to my own fault, and not a reflection of your value, worth or validity. We are all different people, even if we find common experience and solidarity with each other enough to declare trans identity and community.

Contents

Introduction

In the past few years, I've seen the rise of a new kind of sex education resource. Unlike the sex education I – and many of you, I'm sure – received at school, it's less focused on sexually transmitted infection (STI) scares and biological reproduction, and more on pleasure, informing people about their bodies and generally taking a more inclusive approach. It does not just talk about 'men' and 'women' in general terms, but acknowledges that lesbian, gay, bisexual, queer/questioning (LGBQ) and trans people exist. However, I've found myself still frustrated by this kind of inclusion of trans experiences. A gender-neutral version of sex education that focuses on penis-in-vagina sex between people who've never been on hormones or had bottom surgery does include *some* trans experiences, but there are still many trans experiences left out of this narrative. What emergency contraception can somebody on testosterone use? Do erectile dysfunction medications work the same for people on oestrogen? Does a post-vaginoplasty vagina have a g-spot? Why do some people find they enjoy anal sex more after testosterone? Can people with post-surgical vaginas experience vaginismus? These are all questions that gender-neutral versions of cisgender-centred sex education can't answer. When Jessica Kingsley

Publishers approached me, I knew it was my chance to write the book I'd wished had existed for so long.

I wrote this book with the intent of creating a resource for adult trans people to understand our bodies and how we relate to sex, and to answer some questions I've seen come up time and time again in my own trans communities, and dispel some of the myths that are still believed about medically transitioning bodies. However, I also want it to be useful to cisgender people, including the cisgender partners of trans people, so I have tried to write using technical and specific language (which I'm aware may not be the language individual trans people use) in order to make my writing more accessible. I have not written it with the intention of being a 'Trans 101', so it doesn't spend time defining what it means to be transgender or defending the fact that we do, in fact, exist. If you need a more general introduction to trans issues or identity (or want to give it to somebody who needs one), I've listed some more general books in the *Further Resources* section at the end.

We'll cover a lot of ground in this book, from discussing anatomy and hormone replacement therapy (HRT), to talking about specific kinds of sex and kink. I'm a firm believer that good sex education should start with understanding your own experiences of sex, so to begin with we'll dive in to how different people experience desire, pleasure and arousal, as well as why these aren't the same thing. We'll talk about how to navigate sex with other people, including discussion of consent and some of the difficulties that many trans people experience in relation to sex, such as dysphoria and sexual violence.

After that, we'll take a while to talk about physical anatomy, including some specific information about post-hormone or post-surgical anatomy, then about how to engage in safer sex, whether that be related to risks with pregnancy, STIs or erectile dysfunction medication. Other things we'll cover include sex toys (including types of sex toys, how different trans people might want to use them, and material safety) and lube, then we'll focus on specific kinds of sex, including sex using hands, oral sex, vaginal sex and anal sex. Finally, we'll discuss kink, both as part of other more conventional types of sex and as a type of sex in itself. We'll talk about what kink is and look at frameworks around ethics and conduct when it comes to kink, and consent and communication in the context of kink. Finally, there'll also be a *Further Resources* section if you want to do more reading on any of these topics.

I'd like to give a big thank you to Jessica Kingsley Publishers and Andrew James for giving me the opportunity to write this book, and for being incredibly understanding when life events pushed its completion date back. I'd also like to thank my partner for her constant support during the writing process, as well as to my friends for their patience the many times I rescheduled social events in order to find time to write. Finally, I'd like to give a big thank you to the fellow trans people who shared their experiences, knowledge and areas of ignorance with me – you were all invaluable in helping shape this book into what it is.

CHAPTER 1

Desire, Pleasure and Communication

In this first chapter, we'll cover a lot of ground, talking about some of the basics around sex and sexuality, as well as navigating sex with other people.
We'll talk about:

- the differences between desire, pleasure and arousal
- why 'sex drive' doesn't exist
- spontaneous and responsive desire
- brakes and accelerators of sexual desire
- sexual fantasies
- arousal and orgasm
- sexual shame
- consent
- communication
- navigating dysphoria during sex
- navigating sex as a survivor of sexual violence
- abusive relationships.

Desire, pleasure and arousal

Desire, pleasure and arousal are all different things (and all different again from consent). Desire is a want to do something sexual. Pleasure is the positive feelings of happiness and enjoyment that human beings get from particular sensations, including sometimes sexual ones. Arousal is different from pleasure in that it refers to the physiological response to sexual stimuli, such as getting an erection or producing vaginal lubrication.

In a lot of popular culture, we treat the three as connected or even sometimes as the same thing, but they are separate. Somebody can have a desire for sex and experience pleasure from what happens during sex, but not have a physiological response to it. On the flip-side, somebody can be physically aroused but still not have a desire for sex. And none of these things – desire, pleasure or arousal – is the same thing as consent, which is the mutual agreement between parties to have sex. Somebody can desire sexual contact, find what they're experiencing pleasurable and be aroused, and still not consent to sex.

Why 'sex drive' doesn't exist

In a lot of discussions about sex, the term 'sex drive' comes up. Similar to terms like 'hunger drive' and 'self-preservation drive', the term implies that sex is something all humans feel drawn to and that it sits alongside hunger, thirst, warmth and sleep as basic physiological needs. But sex – on a technical level – isn't a drive at all, and on top of that, I think unlearning the idea of sex as a biologically driven need is helpful in understanding the different ways people do (or don't!) feel sexual desire.

That's not to say that sex isn't pleasurable and that a lot of people feel drawn to pleasure – it absolutely is and a lot of people are! But this motivational system isn't quite the same as a drive. For starters, unlike drives such as hunger, an unfulfilled desire for sex doesn't lead to death, and fulfilling a desire for sex can be postponed without impacting somebody's survival.

Uncoupling sexual desire from the idea of a 'drive' is important for two big reasons. First, it ends any implication that there is such a thing as a right to sex – a desire for sex that feels urgent does not mean that somebody has a right to sex with another person, while a person feeling hungry does have a right to adequate food. Second, understanding sex as a drive implies that sexual desire is usually or always spontaneous, when in reality a lot of people experience desire in *response* to arousal.

Spontaneous and responsive desire

So if desire doesn't function as a drive, how do humans feel it? People who feel sexual desire feel it in one of two ways: spontaneously or responsively. (Some people argue that all desire is actually responsive, but that some desires are more mainstream than others and some people may not even recognize the stimuli that they respond to as stimuli, and so experience some of their desires as if they are spontaneous.) Spontaneous desire is the kind of sexual desire that has most cultural emphasis placed on it, to the point where some people may think it's the *only* or 'normal' way to feel desire. Spontaneous desire doesn't exist in response to any kind of stimuli (e.g. being touched in particular ways, or being in a specific kind of environment), and can feel close to a biological drive (which is part of why there's a lot of confusion around 'sex drive'). The other kind of desire – responsive – exists, as the name suggests, in response to external pleasurable stimuli, like kissing or touching or even something like wearing particular materials. People often experience both kinds of desire, although they may lean more heavily towards one or the other, and their primary way of experiencing desire may change over time.

Brakes and accelerators

Once we've laid the groundwork of sexual desire being a motivational system rather than a drive, and that it is sometimes spontaneous and sometimes responsive, we can talk about alternative models of sexual desire beyond the idea of a single 'drive'. The dual control model of desire was developed by Erick Janssen and John Bancroft of the Kinsey Institute in the 1990s, although I was introduced to it through Emily Nagoski's *Come As You Are*. Instead of seeing sexual desire as a single system that ramps up, it sees sexual desire as the result of two systems: the Sexual Excitement System and the Sexual Inhibition System.

The Sexual Excitement System is the accelerator of this metaphor – when it identifies something related to sex (through the senses or in the imagination), it sends signals to the genitals to induce arousal. The Sexual Inhibition System acts as the brakes – if it notices threats in the environment, it sends signals to the genitals to turn off. This isn't necessarily a complete shut down, and in the presence of low-level brake factors, somebody might choose to continue to have sex, but enjoy it less, feel less present in their body, and experience less pleasure.

Specific accelerators vary from person to person, as do brakes. Some examples of what accelerators could look like include particular smells, particular sounds, wearing specific items of clothing or being in a specific environment. Examples of brakes could include knowing an environment is inappropriate for sex (e.g. a work environment), tiredness, worries about STIs or pregnancy, concerns about looking or feeling a particular way, other obligations we have in our lives, or feeling that we aren't living up to societal or social expectations.

Creating space for sexual desire, then, isn't just a case of finding what turns you on (i.e. works as an accelerator), but also finding out what turns you off (i.e. works as a brake). It's also worth knowing that everyone has different levels of sensitivity when it comes to both functions, and that somebody can have a combination of a sensitive or non-sensitive accelerator with sensitive or non-sensitive brakes, with many shades in between, and that these levels of sensitivity (as well as what functions as a brake or accelerator) aren't static, and can shift and change many times over during a lifetime.

Sexual fantasies

One of the key ways that many people discover what they desire from or find interesting about sex is through sexual fantasy. Sexual fantasies are exceptionally common and they often give us room to explore ideas in a safe, controlled environment.

Because of this safe environment – in a sexual fantasy, we have ultimate control – people often fantasize about things they may not necessarily want to do in real life. For example, we may fantasize about sex with STI risks that we would not want to take in real life, with partners we would not want to have sex with in real life, or as genders we don't identify as or want to live as in real life. In some cases, fantasies can involve eroticizing anxieties we have around sex in real life – such as a fear of pregnancy or abandonment – and can therefore be the complete opposite of the kinds of sex we want to have! Sexual fantasies can live exclusively in our heads, be shared with partners or friends, or sometimes be things we *do* want to try in real life.

While sexual fantasies are as varied as people are, they do tend to fall into general categories: sex with multiple partners, sex involving bondage and discipline, sadism and masochism (BDSM), and sex that has a level of novelty to it, acts that have a taboo attached to them, and sex playing with gender and sexuality. Some fantasies fall into multiple categories. While sexual fantasies don't necessarily indicate the kinds of sex we want to have in real life, unpicking and reflecting on them to see what it is we enjoy about fantasies can be useful, both in reducing the shame we have around these fantasies and, in some cases, bringing what we find compelling about them into the real world. This doesn't have to mean bringing it into the real world in its exact form – this can actually be more difficult, as we just don't have the level of control over sex in real life as we do over sex in our heads! For example, you may find that the core of a ravishment fantasy is being too sexually desirable for somebody to resist, or the core of a fantasy you have about having sex with somebody of a gender you're not attracted to is about the novelty of it.

Arousal and orgasm

So if arousal isn't – as we established earlier – the same as desiring sex or finding it pleasurable, what is it? Arousal is a physiological response to external sexual stimuli, which somebody may or may not find desirable or pleasurable. The responses involved in arousal may include erectile tissue (such as in the penis or clitoris) becoming engorged, nipples hardening, blood flow increasing to the genitals, the heart rate quickening, or the body producing more lubrication. In addition to arousal not being necessarily linked to desire, it's worth noting that many of the physiological aspects of arousal may be impacted by medical intervention like hormone replacement therapy or surgery, and the classic 'sexual response cycle' model – where desire leads to arousal, which leads to orgasm followed by resolution – doesn't apply to every sexual situation or every body.

Orgasms vary widely between people, and different orgasms can feel different even to the same person. In the broadest sense, an orgasm is a combination of muscle contractions in the pelvic region and a sudden release of the endorphins oxytocin and dopamine in the brain. Having an orgasm doesn't require genital contact, and some people don't require any contact with their bodies at all to have an orgasm. While some orgasms can feel like an intense 'wave of pleasure', they can also feel gentle, and can vary in duration. Orgasms don't require ejaculation (and ejaculation can happen without orgasm!), and multiple orgasms are possible for people of varying genital and hormonal statuses. However, this requires waiting for what's known as a refractory period – a length of time when we cannot have another orgasm, which can be impacted by things like our hormones.

Culturally, we often treat orgasms as the 'point' of sex, or the ultimate goal of all sex. People may have sex for reasons totally unrelated to wanting an orgasm, such as wanting to feel close to their partner, finding the physical sensations pleasurable even if they don't lead to an orgasm, or even because they are trying to have a baby. Focusing on trying to have an orgasm can actually make it harder to have one, and can make people who are anorgasmic (i.e. cannot have an orgasm) feel broken or 'wrong', which can in turn make it harder to seek help if this is something they want to change.

Sexual shame

A lot of people have a level of shame around sex, be it from the way they were brought up, from having been shamed in the past, or from navigating the world as a marginalized person. For trans people, the way in which we live our lives is often treated as inherently shameful and perverted, even if we aren't engaging in sex or aren't interested in sex at all, and even if we don't come from religious or cultural backgrounds that stigmatize sex and sexuality outside a cisgender (and heterosexual) context. This shame can be exacerbated for those living at the intersection of trans identity and other marginalized identities. Sexual shame can function as one of the sexual inhibitors we talked about earlier. It can act as an internal judgement or conscious silencing of – and stressful feelings about – particular sexual behaviours, desires or fantasies, ways of being touched, or parts of your body.

Navigating and unlearning sexual shame can be a long process, and the exact way to approach it depends on the specific way somebody harbours shame and how it manifests in their sex life. However, there are some ways to grapple with shame that are useful for a wide range of people. First, allow yourself to feel the shame, rather than becoming ashamed that you're ashamed in the first place! We live in a society with a complicated and messy relationship to sex, and it's normal to feel guilt and shame around sex given that we are a product of this society. Giving yourself space to acknowledge these feelings – which can sometimes result in it seeming that things get worse before they get better – is the first step in examining them, identifying the root source (or sources) of shame. Once this root cause (which can sometimes feel like a particular voice, including that of a specific person or institution) has been identified, it can be helpful to build a new micro-community without shame. This micro-community can be made up in many different ways; for example, if you're in a relationship, it may be your partner/s; it could be a support group (in person or virtual); or it could be close friends you trust. A micro-community could even be space you set aside with yourself, or engaging with different social media accounts. Within new shame-free communities, it's possible to find out new information and develop your own, new, healthier values around sex.

Consent

One of the most important things to talk about when it comes to sex is consent. At its simplest, consent in sex means that all parties approve of and agree to sexual acts that are taking place. Sex that takes place without consent from all parties involved is rape or sexual assault.

There are different models of consent, each with their own strengths and weaknesses, ranging from the simple 'no means no' model to the enthusiastic consent model. The enthusiastic consent model is useful for most sexual encounters, and states that consent during sex should be: clear, given freely, enthusiastic, mutual and ongoing. Here, 'clear' means that the people involved should be certain that a person is agreeing to a kind of sexual behaviour, not simply giving an absence of a no; 'given freely' means that the consent should not feel coerced, pressured or given out of fear or in response to a threat; 'enthusiastic' means that all parties should have a level of excitement about sex; 'mutual' means all people involved should give consent; and 'ongoing' means that consent to one act does not necessarily imply consent to a different act. I'd also like to add 'informed consent' as a model of consent, in which everyone is fully aware of what kind of sex they're having, including what risks are associated with it. While it's most commonly used in BDSM communities, I still think informed consent can be a valuable concept outside that context.

While the model of enthusiastic consent works well for most situations, it does have some pitfalls. Somebody can consent to sex they do not have a sexual desire for in a number of circumstances, such as having sex because they are ovulating and trying to get pregnant, or they are engaging in sex work. While 'enthusiasm' does not necessarily mean desire, the cultural narrative around what is 'the normal' way to experience sexuality means that the two often become conflated. Because of this, an alternative model known as the 'authentic consent model' uses the language of 'sincere' rather than 'enthusiastic', specifically to leave space for having sex in these kinds of contexts.

I want to add that sex being consensual does not mean that it is good sex. Additionally, other factors can impact a person's capacity to authentically consent to sex, such as if they have used drugs or alcohol, if they are informed about the risks associated with a particular activity, or if there is a power differential between people.

Some people find the idea of communicating about consent 'awkward', or worry that it will 'kill the mood'. While I would argue that it's more important to be a good partner than to worry about being awkward, I do think part of this idea comes from the way we are taught about consent. We're often taught about it in a way that implies consent is all about learning what not to do or to protect ourselves, rather than as a way for partners to have mutually pleasurable sex, which is what it should be.

Communication

In order to have good sex, it's vital to be able to talk about sex with other people, and the discussion that should take place during sex shouldn't be limited to a first discussion around consent. Nobody is a mind reader, and part of being able to have good sex, touch or intimacy is being able to communicate what kinds of sex, touch or intimacy you want. And identity is not a shorthand for this – being a bottom, a top, stone (disliking particular kinds of touch and/or penetration) or any other kind of sexual identity doesn't inherently mean somebody's desires fall in a particular way, let alone their needs.

Some things are useful to communicate up front, including if you have any areas of your body you don't like being touched, what words you do and don't like being used for your body, what your safer sex boundaries are (see *Chapter 3: Sex and Safety*), and what your turn-ons and turn-offs are. You don't owe anyone an explanation for why your desires and boundaries fall the way they do (although other people do have as much of a right to criticize preferences that fall under and/or reinforce any -isms as you do to have them), and if somebody reacts negatively or refuses when you tell them your boundaries (refusing to use particular words or avoid areas), you might want to rethink whether they're somebody you want to have sex with. It can definitely feel embarrassing at first to talk about sex – especially if you were taught that sex is something shameful – but the important thing is to not treat what you're saying as inherently embarrassing in itself. Telling somebody that you don't want your chest to be touched is likely to feel less daunting if you treat it as a simple fact than if you treat it like a shameful secret. If you need to practise saying what your boundaries and needs are, that's completely okay! Like most things in life, practice makes perfect.

Sometimes, the question of what you want can be difficult to answer, either because you're still ashamed of the answer or because you genuinely don't know what you want. If you feel that you don't know what you want, let alone how to communicate that to somebody else, take some time to think it over in a non-rushed, no-pressure environment. If after that you still don't have an answer, you might choose to pause sex for another time, or to experiment. Either way, communicate with your partner/s, and if you choose to experiment, tell them you'll let them know if you don't like something. If you are experimenting, keep communication going throughout sex. It can also be helpful to not get attached to outcomes – if you feel as if you *need* an experiment to work, it'll be frustrating if it doesn't go the way you planned, but with a more open mind it's easier to take the fact that you *don't* like something as a new finding.

Communication isn't limited to before sex – checking in during and after sex is also really important. The idea that checking in during sex 'isn't sexy' is just as wrong as the idea that getting explicit consent before sex 'isn't sexy' – both show that you care about your partner and want them to be just as comfortable and feel just as much pleasure during sex as you do. This could be asking specific questions – 'Do you like this?' 'Is it better for me to touch here or there?' – or pulling back and taking a moment to pause if you're unsure if somebody is enjoying sex (e.g. somebody goes quite quiet).

Communication also applies to post-sex as well, both in talking about what somebody wants after sex (do they want to wash right away? Do they like pillow talk or want to be left alone?) and in talking about sex after it has happened. Discussing specific things you and your partner/s enjoyed about sex, what you'd like to do again and some things you'd like to try in future can be exceptionally useful. The afterglow of sex can make it feel a lot easier and more comfortable to give each other feedback.

Dysphoria during sex

Gender dysphoria – used as a shorthand for feelings of anxiety and discomfort around the gender/sex somebody was assigned at birth – manifests differently for different people. Some people experience minimal or no discomfort around sex, while others feel it very intensely. It often varies day to day, and somebody may be comfortable having a particular kind of sex one day and absolutely hate it the next.

The most important thing when it comes to navigating sex with dysphoria is to know yourself. Solo sex can be a great way to explore this, thinking about what feels pleasurable, what feels uncomfortable and what makes you feel dysphoric. If you do feel dysphoric, allow yourself to feel these feelings – trying to suppress dysphoria can only exacerbate it. Identify what feels safe or affirming for you – some people find it helpful to focus on an affirming object, like clothing or a prosthetic. Experiment with language internally –what feels affirming, and what makes you feel anxious or uncomfortable? Does it vary depending on situation, and, if so, what situations suit one set of language more than another? Remember that all sex can be adapted, and that sex is a broad category with almost endless variation. If doing something or not being able to do something makes you dysphoric, there might be a way to experience something equivalent or close to it. Bodies don't have to be touched only in specific ways that are gendered – you can touch a chest in ways that feel differently gendered, regardless of what amount and kind of tissue somebody has on their chest.

Once you understand how your dysphoria does or doesn't manifest during sex, communicate with your partner. If somebody has sex with you, they should respect your boundaries. Feelings of dysphoria can be very variable and change quickly, so keep communication honest and open. Remember, you have a right to withdraw consent at any time, and if dysphoria causes sex to stop being pleasurable, you are always allowed to pause or end sex. You do not 'owe it' to your partner/s to keep going.

Navigating sex as a survivor of sexual violence

Transgender people as a group are very likely to experience some form of sexual violence (such as rape, sexual assault or sexual abuse) in their lifetime, and these experiences can make engaging with sex emotionally fraught or difficult, although, as with all traumas, how this manifests depends on the person. Some people find that after experiencing sexual violence, they seek out sexual experiences more, while others have a deep aversion to sex or particular kinds of touch. Sexual violence can also make it more difficult to get physically aroused or experience pleasure, make people far more sensitive to their sexual inhibition system, and feel distanced and alienated from their body.

Focusing on solo sex rather than partnered sex for a while can be really helpful when relearning to occupy your body. Focus on grounding yourself, feeling present in your body. Solo sex can also be helpful in identifying what feels like a 'safe' kind of sexual activity and what triggers you. Many survivors can have trouble reaching orgasm, so instead of focusing on an orgasm, focus on pleasure, relieving some pressure on yourself.

Remember, the point of healing after sexual violence is not to 'go back to the way things were', but to find a new way for you to engage with sex that feels safe and pleasurable. You do not need to enjoy particular kinds of touch, language or sexual acts ever again. If/when you feel comfortable with and desire partnered sex, communicate with your partner/s and take things slowly. And remember to take care of yourself – you are allowed to end, pause or halt sex if you want to.

Abusive relationships

Just as trans people have a higher likelihood of experiencing sexual violence than the general population, we also have a greater likelihood of experiencing domestic and intimate partner violence (IPV), with 54 per cent of the respondents to the 2015 US Transgender Survey saying they had experience of intimate partner violence.[1] While the cultural model we often have of IPV is of cis men committing violence against cis women, people of any gender can be the target or perpetrator of domestic or IPV, and people can be both perpetrator and target at different points in their life. IPV and abuse is not limited to physical abuse, but can include emotional and sexual abuse. Behaviours can include (but are not limited to) using force to intentionally cause pain and discomfort, intentional interference with basic needs by withholding food or medication, the use of coercion and threats, isolating a partner, sexual violence, control over somebody's medical decisions, financial control or minimizing a partner's self-esteem.

While not all abuse that trans people experience in relationships is connected directly to trans status, there are some specific expressions of abuse within trans people's relationships.

For example, a partner may belittle you for your gender identity or expression, threaten to out you, hide your relationship in public, or try to dictate what aspects of transition you should or shouldn't take part in (e.g. tell you that you 'can't' get bottom surgery or 'have to' shave facial hair).

If you are in an abusive relationship, it's important to remember that you are not to blame for your abuse, and abuse is not the result of any actions you have or haven't undertaken. You did not do anything wrong.

CHAPTER 2

Anatomy and Bodies

I n this chapter, we'll discuss some of the variation in anatomy and bodies, as well as some of the many different anatomies that can be created through the medical procedures that some trans people choose to undergo as part of their transition.

We'll talk about:

- ♥ general reproductive anatomy
- ♥ anal anatomy
- ♥ some of the non-medical methods people may use to change the shape of their bodies for gender-affirming reasons
- ♥ the general impact of HRT on genitals and other reproductive anatomy
- ♥ top surgery and post-surgical chests
- ♥ the anatomy of post-bottom surgery genitals.

A lot of our knowledge about medically transitioning bodies is still developing, so some of the information in this book may be outdated as more peer-reviewed research on HRT is carried out and as surgical techniques develop. I also want to give a disclaimer that the anatomies described here are 'averages', especially in the general section. Genitals are as varied as the people who have them, and even among cisgender people there's wide variation in size, shape, form and function. I also don't cover all gender-affirming procedures in this chapter. While the liberation and comfort that some people experience after these procedures *can* have an impact on sex (e.g. people feeling more confident), they're not as directly related/relevant to the scope of this book.

General reproductive anatomy

SEXUAL VARIATION

As mentioned above, the anatomies described in this section are averages, rather than the only ways that bodies can look. Sex is bimodal rather than binary, and there are both a wide variety of ways in which genitals can form and no clear dividing line between particular kinds of genitals. People who are born with bodies that contain features (genitals, gonads, chromosomes, hormones etc.) that don't fit into traditional ideas of 'male' and 'female' or have a mix of features are called intersex people. Intersex bodies don't just look one way, and there are many different forms of being intersex, as well as variation within these forms. Sometimes people are observed as intersex at birth, sometimes they find out they are intersex at puberty, and sometimes they find out even later in life. Some intersex people are able to have biological children, while others aren't.

In this chapter, I sometimes use the word 'homologous', which in this context means that two anatomical features have the same function or develop from the same cells in the foetal stage. We begin life with genitals that have four basic external parts: one that eventually forms the clitoral or penis head (the phalloclitoris), another that forms either a penile shaft or labia minora and clitoral shaft, one that forms the urethra and vagina (if applicable), and a fourth which develops into either labia majora or a scrotum. Intersex conditions that involve variation in external genitals (which is not all intersex conditions) may have an 'atypical' development of any or several of these parts, including having a larger or smaller phalloclitoris than average, a urethral opening in a location more typical of a vulva in somebody with a penis and scrotum, typically 'male' appearing genitalia but with an internal uterus and ovaries, or a vulva but no vagina.

THE VULVA

The term 'vulva' refers to several anatomical features, including the labia majora, labia minora, external clitoris, urethral opening and vaginal entrance.

The labia are the two sets of tissue 'lips' that surround the vaginal opening and urethra. The big outer set are the labia majora. The labia majora are fleshy and have a similar level of sensitivity to normal skin. The labia minora are the inner set of lips. They're made of a different kind of skin to the labia majora, stretch and are responsive to delicate tissues. While representations of vulvas often show neat, even labia minora that can be tucked away inside the labia majora, vulvas in real life have a huge variety of shapes and sizes. It's perfectly normal for labia minora to hang outside the labia majora and for labia to be asymmetrical, with one side hanging lower and/or being larger than the other.

Where the labia minora meet, you can find the clitoris. The clitoris is erectile tissue that's homologous to the penis (in as much as the two can be neatly defined), and doesn't just consist of the external head that's visible when looking at the labia. Instead, the majority of the clitoris is internal, with two 'wings' called the crura, which sit along the pubic bone, and two bulbs that sit on either side of the vaginal opening. The clitoral head is called the glans (like the very head of a penis), and is usually covered by the clitoral hood, a flap of skin that protects the clitoris, much like a foreskin.

Below the clitoris is the urethra, a tiny hole that is where urine comes from. The urethral opening is also the location of the Skene's glands. These glands are also sometimes called the vestibular glands, and produce a milky-white fluid. This fluid can be expelled through the urethra during sex, and is believed to make up part of vaginal ejaculate or 'squirt'.

Below the urethra is the vaginal opening. On either side of the entrance sit the Bartholin's glands, which produce a lubricating fluid in response to arousal.

VAGINAL ANATOMY

The vagina is a muscular canal, made of elastic tissue that expands during arousal (and childbirth); when unaroused, the walls of the vagina actually touch. The average size of the vaginal canal is 2–4 inches when unaroused, although when aroused it expands to 4–8 inches. The shallowest third of the vagina contains the most nerve endings, and different parts of the vagina tend to be sensitive to different types of stimulation. Deeper parts of the vagina tend to be more sensitive to thrusting, while the opening and g-spot tend to be more touch sensitive. The vagina generally ends in the cervix, a cylinder of tissue that connects the vagina to the uterus. Some people have particular areas that are more sensitive than others. These may include the g-spot.

Despite its name, the g-spot is actually not a single spot or a distinct piece of anatomy. Instead, it's an area that contains many tissues, including the crura of the internal clitoris, the urethral sponge and the Skene's glands. Generally, it can be accessed most easily through the vagina, where it's located about 1–2 inches inside the vagina towards the belly. The g-spot tends to have a slightly different texture than the rest of the vaginal lining and may swell during arousal. While not everyone finds g-spot stimulation pleasurable, some people find they are able to ejaculate (or 'squirt') as a result of this.

Technically known as the 'anterior fornix erogenous zone', the a-spot is located around two inches higher than the g-spot, and consists of sensitive tissue between the cervix and the bladder. There is some speculation about whether the a-spot exists, especially as (unlike the g-spot) it doesn't have a different feel to the rest of the vagina. However, most sexologists believe it's real. The a-spot is placed in a similar location to the prostate, and can be indirectly stimulated through anal sex, as well as more directly through vaginal sex.

PENILE ANATOMY

The head of the penis is known as the glans, the same term as the head of the clitoris. It's usually paler than the shaft of the penis, and is where the urethral opening is located. The placement of the urethra is one of the major differences between 'standard issue' penises and vulvas, and one of the things that can be changed with genital reconstruction surgeries. While in 'standard issue' vulvas the urethra sits below the clitoral glans, in most penises the urethral opening (the 'meatus') sits at the tip of the phallus. Some people enjoy urethral stimulation, including penetration, but it can be very sensitive.

The underside of the glans is known as the frenulum, and is also where the foreskin meets the shaft of the penis. The frenulum is often very sensitive, as it contains the highest concentration of nerve endings in the penis. The foreskin is a piece of skin homologous to the clitoral hood, although it is a bit looser and can usually move more easily than the clitoral hood can. The foreskin is sometimes removed for medical, cultural or religious reasons, in a process known as circumcision.

The penis shaft is made of two cylinders of erectile tissue, which enlarge and stiffen with blood during arousal. Because the urethral opening is found at the tip of the glans in most penises, there is also a third cylinder that surrounds it, located on the underside of the penis, known as the 'corpus spongiosum'. This is actually the same tissue that in some people develops into the bulbs of the clitoris!

The scrotum sits underneath the phallus. While the same tissue that forms the labia majora is what can develop into the scrotum, it physically can feel a lot like the labia minora. After puberty, the scrotum contains the testicles, which produce and hold sperm cells. However, before puberty, the testicles are held inside the pelvis, and descend into the scrotum through the inguinal canals. These canals can be used for tucking (see the section in this chapter called 'Non-medical gender-affirming actions') or for a kind of sex called muffing (see *Chapter 5: Manual Sex and Grinding*). The scrotum actually gets thicker during arousal, and the testicles can be drawn closer to the body.

PUBIC HAIR

Pubic hair can vary in growth pattern – while it generally grows on the mons pubis, on the scrotum, on the labia majora and around the anus, it can also grow on the thighs and belly. Generally thicker than the hair on your head, pubic hair can have a variety of textures and level of curl. Different people prefer different styles of grooming when it comes to their pubic hair, and one of the factors that may impact somebody's decision is dysphoria – the presence and/or shape of pubic hair can make somebody's genitals feel more or less prominent, to both them and others.

Anal anatomy

THE PERINEUM

The perineum is technically not part of anal anatomy, but I wanted to include it here. Sometimes known as the 'taint', the perineum is the patch of skin located between the genitals and anus. It's very rich in nerves and can be pleasurable to apply pressure to, use a vibrator on, or massage. Due to its location, the perineum can even be used to stimulate the prostate for those who have them.

THE ANUS AND RECTUM

Just as with the vulva and vagina, the 'anus' is the external part that leads to the internal rectum. Between the anus and rectum there are two sphincters: external and internal. These are strong muscles that control exit and entry to the rectum. The *external sphincter* is the one most people are familiar with, as it's controlled by the central nervous system and so can be clenched or unclenched at will. The external anal sphincter contains a lot of nerves and is sensitive to temperature, pressure, expansion and touch. The *internal sphincter* serves the same biological function as the external sphincter (preventing body waste from exiting the body or anything from entering the body when undesired), but is controlled by the autonomic nervous system rather than central nervous system, so can't be easily manually relaxed in the same way.

These two sphincters sit along the anal canal, which is about 2.5–4 cm long. The anal canal is made of soft skin that can expand significantly, and has a lot of nerve endings, sensitive to touch, temperature and pressure (although the deeper parts of the canal are less sensitive to touch and more sensitive to pressure). Something to note is that the deepest third of the anal cavity consists of a mucous membrane, which absorbs fluid into the bloodstream. Disturbing the outer layer of this membrane can increase the chance of STI transmission (see *Chapter 3: Sex and Safety* to find out more).

Deeper anal penetration extends into the rectum. The rectum is the last stage of the intestines, and functions to absorb excess water from body waste. This means its lining is very absorbent, and potentially more easily damaged or disturbed than the lining of the anus. The rectum also contains fewer nerve endings than the anus, so is generally less sensitive, although it is still sensitive to pressure. The shape of the rectum isn't a straight tube, and instead has two curves, the first tilting forwards towards the belly button and the second tilting back, towards the spine. For some people, these curves can make anal penetration uncomfortable (although the second usually doesn't cause as much discomfort), and the pressure can make somebody feel as if they have to poop. Like the anus, the rectum can expand, although it is more spacious than the anal canal even without expansion. Rectal muscles, unlike anal canal muscles, are not sensitive to temperature, movement or touch, but instead respond to pressure and weight.

The rectum isn't used to store faecal matter, and while some matter may be left behind, pooping should expel most or all of it in the rectum. Penetration deeper than 16–20 cm (using a toy, hand or penis) may pass through the rectum into the sigmoid colon, where faeces are held before they're expelled by the body. While penetration this deep can be pleasurable, it can also require more caution. More force is needed to penetrate that deeply, which can lead to an increased risk of fissures or tearing.

THE PROSTATE

The prostate is a walnut-shaped and -sized gland that some people have wrapped around the urethral canal, between the bladder and penis, and just in front of the rectum. The prostate gland is involved in producing fluid that makes up part of ejaculate, but contains a huge number of nerve endings. The prostate can be stimulated externally through the perineum, but is most easily accessible through the rectum, around 2 inches in and towards the belly button, where it feels like a bulb of tissue. Some people can have an orgasm just from prostate stimulation, although it can take practice and patience. If somebody with a prostate also has a penis, they may not ejaculate during a prostate orgasm, but instead dribble a milky-coloured fluid from their urethra. Oestrogen HRT can cause the prostate to shrink, and some vaginoplasty surgeons position the post-operative vagina so that the prostate can serve as a g-spot.

Non-medical gender-affirming actions

While the actions detailed in this section don't permanently alter anatomy, they still change the shape and visual appearance of bodies and can impact the way in which people want their bodies to be touched and interacted with. Between that and the fact that I make reference to these actions at various points in this book, I thought it was worth inclusion in this chapter.

One disclaimer I want to give is that some of these actions do have health risks. My approach to this is that of harm reduction – for many people, these actions reduce distress and dysphoria to the point where using them is less harmful than not using them. Because of this, I think it's responsible to discuss them and their risks openly, so that people can make informed decisions.

TUCKING

'Tucking' is used to refer to techniques that reduce the visibility of the testes and penis. One of the methods for tucking involves gently pushing the testes up and back into what's called the inguinal canals (two passages in the abdomen that contain the spermatic cords), then pulling the penis and scrotum back between the legs so that they hold the testes in place. Some people prefer to push the testes to the side rather than up, as they find pushing them into the inguinal canals uncomfortable or painful. After this, everything is kept in place using either a specially designed piece of underwear called a gaff, or through tight underwear, shorts or shapewear.

There is – at the time of writing – no published medical research on the risks of tucking. However, we do know about some of the side effects. Use of tape rather than shapewear can cause pain, injury and skin irritation, especially if the tape used isn't medical tape. Tucking can also lead to chronic testicular pain. While there is currently no scientific study of the impact of tucking on fertility, some people have theorized it may have an impact, as the testes need to be at a temperature lower than body temperature to produce sperm, and tucking keeps them close to or inside the body. Tucking too tightly can lead to pain, as the penis becomes cut off from its blood supply, and it can take some experimentation to find a tuck tight enough to minimize the appearance of the penis without causing pain.

Post-phalloplasty people generally *can* tuck, although this is dependent on a few factors and considerations. While it's not possible to push the testes into the inguinal canals in the same way, they can still be moved to minimize their appearance. Some other considerations are that somebody with a semi-malleable erectile implant (see the 'Phalloplasty and metoidioplasty' section of this chapter) may have more difficulty with minimizing the appearance of their penis, and that the average post-phalloplasty penis is larger than the average flaccid penis, so if you know you want to tuck when healed and it's important to you, it may be worth asking your surgeon to create a smaller than average penis.

PACKING

Packing refers to the practice of wearing either padding or a specifically designed object (called a 'packer') in the crotch to create a bulge. Some people differentiate between 'hard packing' (which is used to refer to wearing an object or toy intended for penetrative sex – see *Chapter 4: Toys and Gear*) and 'soft packing', where the padding or object isn't intended for penetrative sex, although 'packing' is often used to just refer to 'soft packing'.

People pack for a variety of reasons, including wanting to alleviate risk of being outed as trans in environments like changing rooms, wanting to subtly change how they sit, walk and move, or because having a bulge makes them feel more comfortable and confident. During sex, some people may want their packer touched and played with as if it's their penis, while others may feel completely happy removing it.

Some packers contain what's known as an STP or 'stand-to-pee' device. This is a funnel that's placed over the urethra and directs urine away from the body, so the person using it can stand up to pee and use urinals. STP devices can also be used during sex – if placed over the vulva, they can transfer the sensation of suction on the end of the STP device onto the vulva. Other specialist packers include 'pack and play' devices, which can be used for penetrative sex due to bendable or insertable rods, and prosthetic packers, which attach to the body with surgical glue instead of being held there by specialist undergarments.

There are very few safety concerns when it comes to packing, other than that of material safety. Cheaper packers can be made of materials called TPE or TPR, which can't be sanitized in the same way that silicone packers can be. This means they can be an STI transmission risk if used for penetrative sex, and unhygienic if used for STP devices. TPE and TPR packers can also 'sweat' the oils used in their manufacturing process, leading to skin irritation and whiteheads, or urinary tract infections (UTIs) if worn directly against the skin. See *Chapter 4: Toys and Gear* for more information on sex toy/prosthetic material safety.

BREAST FORMS

Breast forms are a prosthetic that give people with no breasts or less breast tissue than they'd like the appearance of breasts. They can be made from a wide range of materials, including foam and silicone. Some breast forms are designed for full-day wear, while others aren't as durable, and may be damaged in chlorine water or be at risk of bursting if slept with. Depending on the material, they may be safe to wear against the skin, or may need a layer of cloth in between. Some forms are self-adhesive, while others require the use of medical adhesive strips or glue. The only real risks associated with breast forms (other than wear and tear to the forms themselves) are skin irritation, which can take the form of a rash or peeling, or that if forms are worn directly against the skin, a long-term build-up of sweat and oil can lead to fungal or bacterial infection. This, however, can be mitigated by letting your skin breathe, switching to foam forms overnight if you've been wearing silicone forms, or wearing the silicone forms in a pocket bra so that sweat doesn't pool on the skin.

BINDING

This is the name given to the process of flattening breasts using constrictive materials, with the specialist garments made for this called 'binders'. While binding long term does have some risks associated, such as rib and back pain and difficulty breathing, there are some ways to mitigate some of this risk, and people may decide these risks are minimal compared to the damage of dysphoria if they don't bind. Binding long term can impact the shape and size of breasts, and although there is usually no impact on top surgery viability, it may decrease skin elasticity.

Some people find that they want or need to keep a binder on during sex, may only want their chest touched when they're binding, or may never want their chest touched, even when binding.

Using a specialist binder rather than compression bandages or duct tape is an absolute must for binding in a safer way. These materials don't have the flex required to allow somebody to breathe properly, with compression bandages especially actually tightening, as they're designed to constrict. Another must is minimizing the amount of time spent in a binder – one of the most common pieces of advice is to avoid wearing it for more than eight hours, although how viable this is depends on lifestyle (e.g. work/education hours). Common binder safety advice also includes taking a binder off and wearing a sports bra instead when working out, although this will make exercise completely inaccessible to some people. If somebody experiences pain or difficulty breathing while binding, they should take their binder off straightaway and seek medical advice if their symptoms don't alleviate.

Hormone replacement therapy

In the context of transgender people, hormone replacement therapy (sometimes called 'cross-sex hormone therapy' or CSHT by medical professionals) refers to taking hormonal medication – like androgens, oestrogens and anti-androgens – often with the intention of altering secondary sex characteristics like body and facial hair, breast size, voice, fat distribution and muscle development. The information in this section is generalized, as hormone regimens differ across the world, hormone accessibility may not be constant for any one person, and because even with the same dose, people metabolize hormones in different ways.

Some people use the term 'microdosing' to refer to taking smaller than average amounts of HRT. I don't use this phrase within this section, and instead refer to 'lower doses' where it's relevant. This is for a number of reasons, for example because the phrase is often used for doses that are actually within standard ranges, and a lower dose may be metabolized by somebody more efficiently than a higher dose on a different body and appear to 'work' at the same speed (or quicker!), and smaller doses of hormones often have the same or similar impacts as larger ones would on the same person, just on a different time scale. However, I do want to make it clear that there is no 'one path' of HRT. Different people feel that different doses work best for them; some people may go on hormones for a short while and then come off them, and people of various gender histories may take either or both androgens and oestrogens at various points in their life.

'PUBERTY BLOCKERS'/GNRH AGONISTS

While not technically a kind of CSHT, gonadotrophin releasing hormone (GnRH) agonists – also known as 'puberty blockers', although they can be effective at any point in life – are a kind of medication that impacts hormones and can be taken as part of transition. Examples of GnRH agonists include triptorelin (which is sold under the brand names Decapeptyl® or Gonapeptyl®), goserelin and leuprorelin. These medications prevent the gonads (i.e. the ovaries or testes) from producing sex hormones, which results in the pause of menstruation, prevents additional growth of body and facial hair (and may reduce and thin it), pauses or prevents breast tissue development and reduces sexual desire.

If approved after assessment by a medical specialist (and parental approval if the patient is under the age of 16), GnRH agonists can be taken during puberty – although not usually before a stage of puberty known as Tanner Stage 2, which is when physical development begins – with the aim of 'buying time' for further exploration, reducing the distress of puberty, and possibly reducing the need for other treatments later in life. When GnRH agonists are used in this way, the effects are considered fully reversible.[2] There is some evidence that taking a GnRH agonist without CSHT can have an impact on bone density,[3] so those with a hormone regimen like this should have bone density monitored.

GnRH agonists can also be taken by adults and/or those taking oestrogen or testosterone. While more expensive than anti-androgens like cyproterone, spironolactone and anastrozole, GnRH agonists have fewer side effects. While these are less commonly prescribed for those taking testosterone, some people do take the two together, especially if taking testosterone alone has not stopped their periods.

GnRH agonists are also available as daily nasal sprays, but the most common way to take them is as an injection, administered every four weeks, twelve weeks or six months. While GnRH agonists – like other hormone treatment – should not be counted on as birth control, they can cause temporary infertility, as well as possible erectile dysfunction for those with penises.

OESTROGEN, ANTI-ANDROGENS AND PROGESTERONE

Hormone therapy for transfeminine people often involves three medications: oestrogen, anti-androgens and progesterone. Oestrogen is often taken as a pill or injection, although patches, sprays and gel are also available. However, oestrogen alone is often not enough to suppress testosterone production in the body. A second medication, an anti-androgen, is often taken as well. The specific kind of anti-androgen somebody is likely to be prescribed varies by both region and personal medical history. Spironolactone is commonly prescribed in the US, for example, but in the UK GnRH agonists are much more common. Other anti-androgens that may be prescribed include finasteride and dutasteride. Progesterone is less commonly used in HRT for trans people, although some people do take it. While there's little scientific research to support these claims, many people anecdotally say that progesterone had a positive impact on their mood and energy levels, impacted their body fat redistribution and resulted in better breast development. Progesterone is generally taken as a pill and can also be useful as a partial testosterone blocker.

The effects that these medications have vary by person. Within the trans community, a lot of people refer to taking hormones as a 'second puberty', and just like with a first puberty, the changes that HRT brings can be very slow. Some changes begin within the first three months, while others take much longer. If you're injecting oestrogen, it's important to have good needle safety – see *Chapter 3: Sex and Safety* for information on using needles safely.

Oestrogens change the distribution of fat in the body, can improve mood and cause breast growth. They may also thin facial hair, and cause changes in body odour. Anti-androgens can also prevent additional growth of facial and body hair, and in some cases reduce and thin it. They may also prevent or even reverse some forms of hair loss. Anti-androgens also soften the skin, including skin on the genitals, and weaken muscles, making them smaller. When it comes to sex, oestrogen and anti-androgens can have an impact on fertility, breast growth, arousal and desire, orgasm, seminal fluid, genital sensitivity and size, and there may be difficulty getting or maintaining erections.

While it shouldn't be relied on as birth control, oestrogen can affect sperm production. In some cases, people can produce some sperm after coming off HRT for between three and six months, but the quantity of sperm may be permanently affected. Although not necessarily representative of the entire population, one study[4] found that 4 per cent of its sample of trans women on HRT produced sperm normally in both testicles, and 61 per cent were functionally infertile. We don't have a huge amount of data on the long-term impact of HRT on sperm production, but it still may be worth storing sperm prior to starting HRT if this is something you can afford or have funding for and if you know that having a child is something you want to do.

One of the permanent changes of oestrogen HRT is breast growth. This starts within three to six months of starting HRT, but may take up to or more than three years to reach maximum effect. Tenderness, tingling and sensitivity in the breasts and nipples can be a side effect of this growth, and can make breast touching or fondling uncomfortable or painful. Increased sensitivity of the nipples can mean that people enjoy them more as an erogenous zone, with some people even able to orgasm only from nipple stimulation.

Arousal can feel different for people on oestrogen compared to when they were pre-HRT, with some people reporting this as arousal feeling more 'whole body' compared to genital only. Some people find that their desire for sex decreases on oestrogen, while others find that an increased sense of connection to their body actually increases their desire for sex. Lots of people also say that progesterone increases their desire for sex, although again there is insufficient research data on this. HRT can also impact the way an orgasm feels, making it again more of a 'whole body' experience. Some people find that multiple orgasms become easier on HRT and that their orgasms produce little or no fluid.

On HRT, ejaculate changes in terms of consistency, volume, colour and taste. When testicles atrophy on HRT, the Cowper's gland – responsible for pre-ejaculate fluid – becomes one of the primary sources of fluid. This has a watery, thinner and clearer consistency than semen, and may 'leak' or drip when the person is orgasming and/or aroused.

HRT can cause the penis to become more sensitive, and decrease in size, and may cause difficulty gaining or main-taining erections. In some cas-es, erections can become pain-ful on HRT. This phenomenon hasn't been studied enough, and while there is some gener-al folk wisdom around it (usu-ally that it's due to a lack of spontaneous erections mean-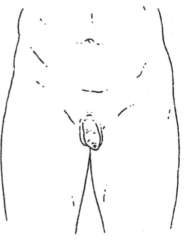ing people experience fewer regular erections than necessary for penile tissue health), we still don't really know the mechanisms behind this. Erectile dysfunction medication is safe for those on HRT (see *Chapter 3: Sex and Safety* for information on using them safely), and some people use genital pumps or topical testoster-one in order to slow or prevent a decrease in size. Many people swear by a 'use it or lose it' approach, where having regular erec-tions prevents both shrinkage and pain, although as with many things in transition, your experience may be different.

TESTOSTERONE

Testosterone (T) is usually taken on its own, without an anti-oes-
trogen. It can be taken as a gel, as patches or as an injectable,
with different forms and doses requiring different frequencies of
administration. In some cases, people choose to take testosterone pellets, which are around the size of a grain of rice and are
implanted under the skin (subdermally). However, pellets are a
generally rare method of administration, as they require local
anaesthetic and have to be replaced every three to six months.
While oral testosterone has been used by trans people in the
past, it is rarely prescribed today, as oral testosterone is linked
to liver damage.

As with oestrogen, the changes that T brings vary by person, especially in terms of time, and it can take many years to
reach the full effect, as with any kind of puberty. In many cases,
unwanted effects can be mitigated (e.g. waxing or even laser hair
removal can be used to get rid of unwanted body or facial hair),
but there are alternative pathways to achieving some changes,
like voice (which can be trained) or facial hair (which even some
cis women have, and which can be encouraged with minoxidil
even when pre- or non-T). It can be helpful to look at cis male
relatives to predict some of the results of taking T, but even then
there's a ton of variation between people, and the effects given
here are general rather than guaranteed.

Some of the physical changes that T can bring include the
growth of facial and body hair, a lowered voice pitch, a change
in body odour, a change in fat distribution, an increase in muscle
mass and, in some cases, shrinkage of breast tissue (although T
can't get rid of breasts entirely). Many (but not all) people find
that T stops their periods, and a lot of people – depending on

when they start taking T – also report their feet increasing in size and width. When it comes to sex, some key impacts of T are changes to fertility, sexual desire and arousal, changes to the orgasm, bottom growth, vaginal atrophy, and sometimes pelvic pain.

While taking T doesn't necessarily make a person infertile, it can make getting pregnant more difficult. That said, T alone should not be relied on for birth control, and if somebody is having sex with a risk of pregnancy that they want to avoid, they should use additional methods of contraception, such as condoms, the copper coil and so on (see *Chapter 3: Sex and Safety*).

Some people find that testosterone CSHT increases the way they experience sexual desire and arousal, feeling spontaneous desire more frequently. While there are no studies about this, some people on T also report *who* they are sexually attracted to changing when on T, although this could easily be the result of newly found sexual confidence rather than T itself. T can also change how people feel their orgasms, making them more genital-centred rather than convulsive, making it quicker and easier to achieve orgasm, and reducing the desire for multiple orgasms.

'Bottom growth' or clitoral growth is sometimes one of the first changes that people experience on T, although it can also take a few months or even years to begin for others. Clitoral growth is permanent, so even if somebody later goes off testosterone, they will still maintain their size.

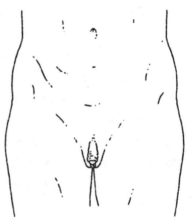

Bottom growth size depends heavily on the person, although the average size is about 1–2 inches in length when erect. When the clitoris is growing, some people can find they experience discomfort, especially if they're packing or their underwear rubs on their bottom growth.

While there is (at the time of writing) no studies that prove it has any impact, some people choose to pump their genitals to try and increase size, and others take DHT (dihydrotestosterone, another androgenic hormone) for the same reason. While individual preferences vary, some people enjoy their bottom growth being focused on during sex (solo or partnered) and/or enjoy the sensation of it being 'jacked off'. In some cases, people have large enough bottom growth that they can use it for penetrative sex (although this is also dependent on body shapes, size and flexibility levels), with some sex toys specifically made to simulate this.

Vaginal atrophy is the technical term for vaginal tissues becoming thinner and dryer, which is related to a drop in oestrogen levels. Because it's related to a decline in oestrogen levels rather than simply an increase in testosterone, it's relatively easy to mitigate – a topical oestrogen cream or vaginal ring can be applied or inserted into the vagina without impacting overall hormone levels. Other treatment options include anti-inflammatory medication and muscle relaxants.

Vaginal atrophy can mean that people on T don't produce as much natural lubrication as those not on T, and so have a greater need for lube. Using lube also decreases the risk of bleeding as a result of breaking thinner vaginal tissue, which becomes more prone to microabrasions. Other issues linked to vaginal atrophy are UTIs – people on T have an increased likelihood of UTIs, especially if they bottom for penis-in-vagina sex. Antibiotics can be used to treat UTIs, but if somebody is having recurring UTIs, a course of vaginal oestrogen can be helpful.

Pelvic or abdominal pain is a symptom that we don't currently know a huge amount about, but that seems to impact a significant number of people on testosterone. For some people this pain may be cyclical, whereas for others it may be brought on by eating food or having an orgasm. There are some treatment options. Anecdotally, many people have found that their pain decreased after they increased their dose of T, although this hasn't been studied in a scientific setting. Alternatively, some people choose to undergo a hysterectomy and/or oophorectomy to remove the cause of this pain.

Top surgery

'Top surgery' is a slang term used within trans communities to refer to surgeries that change the shape of the chest. While 'top surgery' is sometimes used specifically to refer to mastectomy, other surgeries like breast reduction and breast implants are included under this umbrella.

BREAST AUGMENTATION
Breast augmentation (or breast implantation) involves the use of implants – saline or silicone – to enhance the shape, size or volume of breasts. Breast augmentation is a very common form of plastic surgery, although some surgeons do have slight differences in the surgical techniques they use for cis and trans women. Generally, chest sensation does return after breast

augmentation, although it can take up to 12–18 months for full sensation to be regained. As with other forms of top surgery, regaining sensation can temporarily feel painful, be it a burning sensation or sharp, shooting pain. The chance of total nipple sensitivity loss is extremely low, but if no sensation has returned within two years of surgery, it's unlikely it will return at all.

Breast implants – once healed – are generally very sturdy. Repeated rough manipulation – including impact play or bondage – can eventually result in rupture, but this is generally quite rare. If you know you want to play in a heavy way, it's worth talking to a surgeon about implant safety prior to undergoing surgery. Alternatively, it's completely fine to decide this isn't something you want to risk, and stick to lighter or other forms of play.

BREAST REDUCTION

Some trans people choose to have breast reduction surgeries, sometimes instead of mastectomy and in other cases for the same health-related reasons that cis women have for choosing breast reduction (e.g. back pain). The types of incisions made vary by patient and surgeon, but the most common is anchor-type incisions, which can also be used to create flat chests for those with smaller breasts. This technique generally does not involve removing the nipples or severing the nipple stalk, so nipple sensitivity is regained post-surgery. However, in some cases reduction may require free nipple grafts. This refers to the process by which nipples are removed, and then grafted back onto the chest. This can lead to the loss of the nipple or permanent loss of nipple sensation. Even when nipples aren't removed, changing their position can cause temporary loss of nipple sensitivity, which in some cases can be permanent. That said, some people actually report an increase in nipple sensitivity following breast reduction.

Double incision mastectomy top surgery can be carried out after breast reduction, although the placement of scars and potential removal of skin during breast reduction can impact top surgery outcomes and change some surgical techniques. Excess skin in the central chest area can require joined double incisions, for example. If free nipple grafts were carried out during breast reduction, the nipples can be relocated and resized.

DOUBLE INCISION MASTECTOMY

Also sometimes called bilateral mastectomies, these are the most common type of top surgery for those seeking removal or reduction of the chest. It involves making two incisions – hence the name – on the top and bottom of the pectoral muscle, pulling back the skin, and removing the breast tissue. The scars from this can have a huge variety of appearances, dependent on the incisions that a surgeon made, sun exposure, a person's body shape and size, age of the scars, stretching during healing, and if somebody is prone to keloid scarring – not all double incision top surgery scars look like neat pink lines under pectorals.

As part of a double mastectomy, some people choose to have free nipple grafts. Because this involves severing the nerves that connect to the nipple, some people find they have little feeling in their nipples after top surgery. Additionally, there is a risk that grafted nipples will not take and will be lost. This risk increases for those who smoke, people with diabetes or people with auto-immune diseases. Not everyone chooses to have their nipples regrafted, with some opting to undergo medical tattooing to make them appear as if they have nipples; others wear prosthetic nipples, or get the entire area tattooed to make it less noticeable.

While sensation can be temporarily lost post-surgery, most people regain sensation in their chests 6–12 months after surgery. People who have top surgery, still menstruate and experience chest tenderness as a pre-menstrual symptom may find their tenderness diminished or completely gone after top surgery.

T-ANCHOR, KEYHOLE AND PERIAREOLAR TOP SURGERY

Like double incision mastectomies, t-anchor, keyhole and peri-areolar top surgery techniques involve the removal of breast tissue. However, these techniques do not involve removing nipples (even though they can involve resizing the nipples), meaning that nipple sensation is largely retained. However, periareolar and keyhole surgery have some limitations in that they can only be used on people with small chests and good skin elasticity.

Bottom surgery

ORCHIECTOMY AND HYSTERECTOMY

Orchiectomy and hysterectomy are surgical procedures that remove part of the internal reproductive system (the testicles and uterus – and sometimes also the ovaries, fallopian tubes and cervix). Hysterectomy and orchiectomy are sometimes carried out as part of or prior to another kind of genital reconstruction surgery (e.g. metoidioplasty or vulvoplasty), but are also often carried out on their own.

ORCHIECTOMY

Orchiectomy is the term for a surgery that removes one or both testicles. Unlike another procedure, called a scrotectomy, orchiectomies don't remove all or part of the skin that makes up the scrotum. This means that scrotal tissue is still available for construction into the vulva or vagina if you later choose to have vulvoplasty and/or vaginoplasty.

One of the biggest impacts that orchiectomies have is on HRT. After a bilateral orchiectomy, the body no longer produces testosterone, so an anti-androgen is no longer needed. Some people find they can also reduce their oestrogen doses after an orchiectomy. Another significant impact it has is on fertility. While post-orchi people can still ejaculate some (often clear-ish) fluid, they no longer produce sperm. Desire for sex can also drop, with some people who dislike this choosing to take small doses of testosterone. Removal of the testicles means that taking some kind of hormone treatment is compulsory for life, with a high risk of osteoporosis and other bone diseases otherwise.

HYSTERECTOMY

Hysterectomy is the surgical removal of the uterus, and for trans people is often undertaken alongside salpingo-oophorectomy (removal of the ovaries and fallopian tubes) and the removal of the cervix. Some people choose to have a hysterectomy during phalloplasty or metoidioplasty, some prior to these surgeries, and some as an alternative. The reasoning behind wanting a hysterectomy varies, with some people finding it affirming of their gender, others wanting to remove the chance of future pregnancy and completely stop periods, and others simply wanting it as part of other bottom surgery. Hysterectomy usually does not involve the removal of the vagina (vaginectomy).

Historically, there has been a recommendation from some doctors that hysterectomy and oophorectomy are undertaken within the first five years of starting testosterone therapy, but this absolutely is not compulsory. The theory behind this recommendation is that when testosterone suppresses periods, this causes a thickening of the lining of the uterine wall (known as endometrial hyperplasia), which can then lead to an increased cancer risk. However, studies haven't shown any increased risk of reproductive cancers from taking testosterone.

After a hysterectomy, some people find they can decrease their testosterone doses or (if they have had their ovaries removed) find that the effects of T become more pronounced. As with orchiectomies, taking some kind of hormone treatment is required following an oophorectomy, in order to reduce risk of osteoporosis.

Having a hysterectomy can impact orgasms – while it doesn't mean somebody can't have an orgasm, those who experienced more intense uterine contractions during their orgasms may find them to be less intense afterwards. There are conflicting opinions on the impact of cervix removal on orgasms. Some people can find they have less sensation as a result of vaginal penetration after hysterectomy.

VAGINOPLASTY AND VULVOPLASTY
VAGINOPLASTY

Vaginoplasty (in the context of trans healthcare at least) is a surgical procedure that creates a vagina and vulva by reconstructing a penis and scrotum. In some cases, somebody might choose to just have a vulva constructed, which is known as a 'zero-depth vaginoplasty' or vulvoplasty.

There are other vagino-plasty methods than the ones discussed here (e.g. skin graft), but they are significantly less common. Vaginoplasty can be done in one or two stages, with the second stage usually being labiaplasty, a cosmetic revision of the labia created in the first stage. The size of a post-vagi-noplasty vagina depends on a number of factors, including the technique chosen, somebody's pre-op anatomy, and how post-op results have healed. On average though, a post-op vaginal canal has a depth of 4–6 inches, compared to cis women's average depth of 3–6 inches. It is completely untrue that people who have not gone through puberty due to taking GnRH agonists ('puberty blockers') are unable to have vaginoplasty.

Internal sensation can vary by surgical technique and recovery, but most post-vaginoplasty people are able to orgasm, and some people who were unable to orgasm prior to surgery may find themselves able to afterwards. The prostate is almost always left in place, and in most cases the vaginal canal is placed so that the prostate is anterior to the vagina, in a similar position to the g-spot. Post-vaginoplasty clitorises can be larger than average, and may or may not have a clitoral hood depending on the surgeon's technique.

Post-vaginoplasty vaginas have similar microbiomes to the

vaginas of cis women.[5] Some people use the term 'neo-cervix' to refer to the tissue at the deepest part of a post-op vagina. While this is made of a different kind of tissue to cis women's cervixes and is associated with a much lower risk of cancer, there is still a small risk of developing vaginal or cervical cancer post-vaginoplasty, so coming up with a plan for cancer screening with your GP or primary care physician is important.

PENILE INVERSION

Penile inversion vaginoplasty is the most common form of vaginoplasty. It involves the creation of the vaginal lining from penile skin, with the labia majora made from the scrotum, and the penis glans used to create a clitoris. Some people find that they do secrete some fluid from their Cowper's glands (which produce pre-cum when pre-op) when they are post-op, and may not need additional lubrication depending on how much fluid they produce. However, even if somebody does produce fluid, it may not be enough for comfortable penetration, and some people don't have any self-lubrication. As with many things in trans healthcare, your experience may be different.

If there isn't enough tissue in the penis alone, a surgeon may carry out a 'penoscrotal flap technique', which also uses tissue from the scrotum. This can make penile inversion vaginoplasties available to those who have experienced genital atrophy on HRT, or who have been on GnRH agonists during puberty.

SIGMOID COLON PROCEDURE

An alternative method of vaginoplasty uses a section of the sigmoid colon to create the new vaginal canal. This is sometimes used to repair complications of an existing vaginoplasty, or for people who don't have enough penile and scrotal tissue for a penile inversion vaginoplasty. Because it doesn't utilize the tissues of the penis, it can be used as part of a penile preserving vaginoplasty. This surgery is less common than penile inversions, as the surgical risks are higher, due to both the time the surgery takes and the fact it involves intestines.

This method does generally result in a vagina that self-lubricates, although it's not completely guaranteed. Anecdotally, some people find their vagina creates too much lubrication, and have to wear pads or panty liners. Additionally, while the biome (and resulting smell) of a post-op vagina does generally shift to be similar to that of a cis woman's vagina, this can take time and it may smell odd or unpleasant in the meantime.

PENILE PRESERVING VAGINOPLASTY

While newer and less common, colon and scrotal tissue vaginoplasty procedures can be used in vaginoplasty procedures that still preserve somebody's already existing penis. If colon tissue is used, somebody could also keep their testicles and scrotum, although this would mean potentially less tissue and less room to create the vulva. With penile preserving vaginoplasty, the urethra can either be re-routed or left in the penis. Some people who have penile preserving vaginoplasties use topical testosterone gel to help with getting and maintaining erections. It is possible to tuck after penile preserving vaginoplasty, although there are some changes in penis positioning.

DILATION

After vaginoplasty, dilation is needed to keep the vagina open. This involves placing a tube-shaped device into the vagina, and holding it there for a specified amount of time. The idea that a post-op vagina will 'heal closed' if somebody doesn't keep dilating is a myth, and one often utilized in transmisogynistic ways. Once the initial healing period is over, dilation is a muscle training exercise, just as it is for people with non-op vaginas who use dilators (e.g. because of vaginismus). Some people can lose some depth (which can be permanent) as their vagina contracts, but it will not 'seal itself shut'. While dilation can be multiple times a day during the early days, after healing some people find they only need to dilate once a week. In many cases, having penetrative sex or masturbating with a dildo may suffice, although this is something somebody should check with their surgeon.

VULVOPLASTY

Unlike vaginoplasty, vulvoplasty does not involve the creation of a vaginal canal. Instead, it involves creating a labia and clitoris, although in most cases a shallow dimple (the 'vaginal introitus dimple') can be created, which is sometimes also known as shallow-depth vaginoplasty. Some people choose vulvoplasty over vaginoplasty because they have multiple risk factors, don't want to commit to dilating or they're uninterested in receiving vaginal penetration. Somebody who's had a vulvoplasty can later choose to have a full-depth vaginoplasty, but it must be done using skin grafts or a section of sigmoid colon.

PHALLOPLASTY AND METOIDIOPLASTY

Phalloplasty and metoidioplasty (sometimes called phallo and meta) are two different types of genital surgery that construct a penis. While there are some significant differences between the two types of surgery, they do have a lot of procedures (or potential procedures) in common. These procedures include vaginectomy, urethroplasty (or 'urethral lengthening'), and scrotoplasty.

Vaginectomy refers to the removal of the vaginal canal and closure of the opening. This is not normally done as its own procedure outside the context of either phalloplasty or metoidioplasty, but it can be done as a stand-alone procedure. Vaginectomy can impact orgasms, as contractions felt in the vagina will be lost, although this doesn't mean somebody will lose the ability to have them.

Urethroplasty is an optional part of phalloplasty and metoidioplasty that creates a new urethra that is longer and repositioned compared to the existing one, which is then 'hooked up' to somebody's existing urethra. This involves using tissue taken from a donor site, such as the vaginal lining or cheek.

Scrotoplasty involves the creation of a scrotum using the labia and either silicone implants or part of a pump system (see the 'Phalloplasty' section below). Scrotoplasty can be carried out with or without vaginectomy, although is almost never carried out as a stand-alone procedure. Depending on the specific technique used, scrotoplasty may involve creating one scrotum by rotating the labia upward and joining them (VY), or leaving the labia in their existing position, but joining them in the middle (simple). If somebody doesn't have a vaginectomy, their vagina will be behind their balls after a VY scrotoplasty and between them after a simple scrotoplasty. It is possible to have a VY scrotoplasty after a simple scrotoplasty.

Not everyone who has phalloplasty or metoidioplasty has all of these procedures; for example, some people choose to have phalloplasty with scrotoplasty but without vaginectomy, while others might choose to have a metoidioplasty with vaginectomy but without urethral lengthening. Reasons for choosing particular options may include wanting to minimize some of the risks of bottom surgery, not feeling a want for particular functions, or wanting to minimize future upkeep procedures. Different surgery teams may have different levels of comfort with particular combinations of procedures, but they are possible.

That said, there are some complications associated with particular combinations of surgical options. Having a urethroplasty without a vaginectomy can increase the chance of fistulas, for example, as surgeons won't be able to reinforce the 'hook-up site' with tissue from the vaginal lining. Another example is that somebody who has scrotoplasty but no vaginoplasty may find vaginal penetration difficult and need to dilate.

PHALLOPLASTY

Phalloplasty creates a penis using a graft of skin taken from somewhere on the body, most commonly the forearm (known as radial forearm free flap – or RFFF – phalloplasty) or thigh (anterior lateral thigh – or ALT – phalloplasty). The size of the post-op penis is dependent on a few factors, including patient preference, 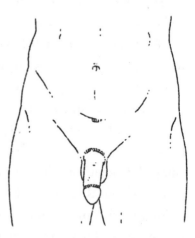 surgeon comfort and what donor site is available. One consideration is that post-phalloplasty penises remain the same size whether flaccid or erect, unlike cis men's penises.

Phalloplasty is a multiple-stage procedure, with surgeries potentially spread out over a year or more. Different surgery teams include different procedures in different stages, although generally stage 1 involves the creation of a new penis and urethra (if urethroplasty is chosen) from a skin graft; stage 2 involves sculpting of the glans of the new penis, clitoral burying (an optional procedure, in which the clitoris is moved to the base of the new penis, increasing sensation) and/or nerve hook-up, and urethral hook-up, scrotoplasty and vaginectomy, if applicable. Stage 3 involves the (again, optional) implantation of an erectile device. Another procedure that may be included in phalloplasty is nerve hook-up, a microsurgery where nerves from the donor tissue are connected to nerves in the pelvis or clitoris.

Because so many of the procedures within phalloplasty are optional, post-phalloplasty genitals can be widely diverse in appearance. Somebody who has chosen not to undergo clitoral burying will have a clitoris in addition to their penis, somebody who has chosen not to have scrotoplasty will not have testicles, and somebody who has chosen not to have vaginectomy will still have a vagina. This diversity also applies to sensation and function – it's very rare to have no sensation, and with a nerve hook-up it's possible to have erotic sensation throughout the entire penis, but it can take up to two years for this to develop. Sensation may be uneven throughout a post-phallo penis, and if the clitoris is buried in the new penis, this often means that the base of the penis is more sensitive.

While post-phalloplasty penises can't ejaculate sperm, people who find they can 'squirt' pre-phallo sometimes find that they ejaculate the same clear fluid through their post-phalloplasty penis if they've had urethral lengthening, as the Skene's glands (where this fluid is produced) aren't removed during vaginectomy. As post-phalloplasty penises can be a single shade and often lighter than a cis man's penis would be, some people choose to undergo tattooing, once their penis has healed, to pigment the area.

ERECTILE IMPLANTS

Many – but not all – people who undergo phalloplasty choose to have an erectile implant. Post-phalloplasty penises cannot achieve erection on their own, and while not everyone who undergoes phalloplasty is interested in using their penis for penetrative sex, those who are will have one of two main types of prosthesis implanted: malleable or inflatable. Neither allows for spontaneous erections.

Malleable implants consist of a bendable steel core, covered in silicone, which allows the penis to be moved to an erect or flaccid position. These implants are cheaper than inflatable implants and can last for a much longer time without requiring replacement. However, they do result in a penis that feels semierect all the time, which can look and feel awkward for people.

Inflatable implants involve a system of two silicone cylinders in the penis shaft, a reservoir of saline and a hydraulic pump that moves saline from its reservoir to the cylinders, causing an erection. In both two-piece and three-piece inflatable implants, the hydraulic pump is located in one of the testicles, replacing a simpler silicone implant. In two-piece implants, a penis is returned to flaccid by bending the penis to deflate it, while in three-piece implants, a release valve in the pump in the scrotum is pressed. These implants result in a penis that is easier to conceal under clothing than one containing a malleable implant,

66

and erections can feel more 'natural' using them. However, these implants have a higher rate of failure and may need replacing more frequently and quickly than malleable implants.

METOIDIOPLASTY

Metoidioplasty doesn't involve using a skin graft to create a new penis, like phalloplasty. Instead, it uses already existing clitoral growth from testosterone to create a penis. It involves detachment of the clitoral ligaments, which causes the clitoris to drop position and appear longer. If this is the only procedure 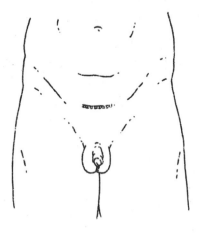 involved in a metoidioplasty, it's sometimes called a 'simple meta' or 'simple clitoral release'. However, as with phalloplasty, other procedures like vaginectomy, urethroplasty and scrotoplasty may be included within metoidioplasty. Somebody can choose to have metoidioplasty and then go on to have phalloplasty. One procedure that sometimes is carried out as part of a metoidioplasty is a mons resection. This is similar to a tummy tuck, but carried out lower on the body with the intention of making a post-op penis more visible.

Unlike phalloplasty, metoidioplasty can be done in a single stage, although in some cases scrotoplasty is carried out as a second stage. Another difference between the two is that metoidioplasty doesn't involve an erectile implant, as the post-op penis utilizes the erectile tissue that was previously in the clitoris. Metoidioplasty does result in a penis that is smaller than a post-phalloplasty penis, with an average size of 1–3 inches. Some people find they can't penetrate a partner with their post-op penis, while others can – it may be difficult to find condoms the right size, so you may need to find custom-sized condoms, or use internal condoms (see *Chapter 3: Sex and Safety*). It's extremely unlikely that you'll lose the ability to orgasm after metoidioplasty – in fact, one survey[6] of multiple metoidioplasty studies found that all of its participants retained erogenous sensation after surgery.

Sex and Safety

I n this chapter, we will talk about safety around and during sex. This is an incredibly broad topic, but our focus will primarily be about the risks of STIs and pregnancy, although we'll also briefly discuss emotional safety (see *Chapter 1: Desire, Pleasure and Communication* for a more in-depth discussion of emotional safety).

We'll talk about:

- ♥ 'safe sex' vs 'safer sex'
- ♥ safer sex boundaries
- ♥ talking about safer sex
- ♥ some of the different kinds of STIs
- ♥ how to mitigate STI transmission risk
- ♥ pre-exposure prophylaxis (PrEP) and post-exposure prophylaxis (PEP)
- ♥ getting tested
- ♥ the impact of HRT on pregnancy risk
- ♥ how to mitigate pregnancy risk
- ♥ what to do if your mitigations don't work
- ♥ accessing abortion services when trans
- ♥ using Viagra and other erectile dysfunction drugs safely.

While safety in sex tends to be a primary (if not *the* primary) focus of sex education, I still wanted to dedicate a chapter to it in this book for a number of reasons. The first is that while sex education does tend to focus on safety, this does not mean that the information presented within all sex education is accurate. This is an issue even for cisgender people; between 2011 and 2013, 43 per cent of teenage girls and 57 per cent of teenage boys in the US did not receive any information about birth control before they had sex for the first time.[7] There are plenty of places across the world where the only sex education available is abstinence-only programmes that don't provide accurate – if any – information on mitigating sexual risks.

A second reason is that, despite the focus on sex and safety in mainstream sex education, transgender people still lack specific resources. When sex education is created about cisgender bodies and for cisgender people, it does not address trans-specific concerns even if it's gender neutralized. For example, despite transgender people being an at-risk population for HIV, PrEP dosing recommendations are often created with cisgender people in mind and – at the time of writing – specific dosing recommendations for post-bottom surgery people do not exist at all. When barrier methods are recommended, this does not address the fact that conventional condoms may not fit post-metoidioplasty people. Trans-specific resources on safer sex are necessary!

'Safe sex' vs 'safer sex'

Something I want to highlight at the start of this chapter is that I'll be referring to 'safer sex' rather than 'safe sex'. While 'safe sex' is the more common term, it's not accurate – no type of sex can ever be free of risk. I don't say this in order to scaremonger, but to emphasize that methods of mitigating risk are just that – ways of mitigating the risk, not removing it entirely. There is nothing in life that's without risk, but we just learn to mitigate risk to an acceptable level. If we cross the road, for example, we learn to do it at a crossing and after looking to see if vehicles are coming. In the same way, if we decide to have sex, we should learn to do it after taking whatever measures we want or need to reduce risk to a level that's acceptable to us.

What's important to remember is that you have a right to decide what level of risk you're alright with taking and what your boundaries are. For one person, this might mean they're uninterested in any kind of oral, hand or penetrative sex without a barrier (like condoms, dental dams or gloves), while for another this might mean they take PrEP and are happy to have sex without barriers if there's no pregnancy risk; for others, it might mean they only have sex within a monogamous relationship.

Another thing to emphasize is that contracting an STI or having a pregnancy scare does not reflect on somebody's value or worth. Contracting an STI doesn't make somebody 'dirty', and birth control failing doesn't make them a bad person. If the steps you have taken to mitigate risk fail, this is not a moral failing; it is a health condition.

Safer sex boundaries

When it comes to safer sex there are two major things to remember. The first is that you have a right to decide what level of sexual risk you are willing to engage with, as well as what steps to mitigate risk you are or aren't comfortable with. The second is that you have a responsibility to make clear what level of sexual risk you are comfortable with and what steps you are/aren't taking to mitigate risk with your partner/s, in order for them to make an informed decision about whether this is within their own limits for acceptable risk.

For example: Person A may get an STI screening every month and take PrEP, but otherwise not use any other method of risk mitigation, such as using barriers. While their actions do make the risk of HIV transmission very low, there are other transmission risks to take into account, as well as possibly the risk of pregnancy. If Person A wants to sleep with Person B, it is their responsibility to communicate this background information to Person B so that Person B can make an informed decision about whether this level of risk is something they're willing to accept.

FIGURING OUT YOUR SAFER SEX BOUNDARIES

Your safer sex boundaries are yours to define; no two people have exactly the same boundaries, and what your boundaries are will likely change over your life, be this because of changing tastes in sex and play, changing relationship status, changing sense of health or for a variety of other reasons.

But how do you figure out your safer sex boundaries? Like anything, through thinking and experimenting. What would make you feel emotionally safe? Would you like to reserve particular kinds of sex for particular kinds of relationship? Is there a particular way of being touched that would make you feel uncomfortable or unsafe? Would a partner being on PrEP be enough for you to feel comfortable having sex without barriers? Would you like partners to get tested before you start having sex with them?

If all these questions seem overwhelming, something that could be helpful is a yes/no/maybe list. You and your partner/s can discuss different acts, your desires around them (including how you'd like to engage with them), whether the risks involved in them are risks you're willing to take under any circumstances (yes), not risks you're willing to take (no), or risks you're willing to take under particular circumstances (maybe). If something is a 'maybe', take the time to think about what those particular circumstances are.

Some of your boundaries may seem arbitrary, and it's okay if that's the case! Feelings do not abide by logic, and decisions about what mitigations we need or want are based on our feelings of comfort. For what it's worth, I have boundaries when it comes to emotional or physical safety that are incredibly arbitrary! While you can negotiate boundaries with partners if you want to, at the end of the day your boundaries are defined by you.

That said, it can be helpful to leave yourself room for those boundaries to change in the future. A kind of sex that feels emotionally safe at one point in life may not later, or as you become more educated on physical risks, you may be willing to use different mitigation strategies. For example, a person might insist on using barriers for all sex, while later in life they might choose to go on PrEP instead. Another example is kink play or BDSM (read *Chapter 9: Kink* for a more detailed discussion of this); as somebody becomes more educated about the subject and gains more experience with rope, they might be more willing to take on the risk of rope suspension.

Of course, sexual partners are not mind readers. Once you've figured out what your boundaries are when it comes to sexual risk and safer sex, you then have a responsibility to communicate these boundaries to your partner/s.

Talking about safer sex

So once you've figured out what your sexual boundaries are, how do you get your partner(s) on the same page?

The answer will be somewhat different depending on what kind of relationship you have with your partner(s). Discussions of anything within a relationship will be different if it's a one night stand compared with if it's a long-term relationship. That said, there are some tips for bringing up safer sex that can be helpful no matter what kind of relationship you have.

The best time to talk about safer sex practices is before you have sex. However, if you've already had sex before having a full conversation about safer sex, the next best time is as soon as possible after having sex, although you may need to change some of the questions you're asking. It can be helpful to offer your own information first – this can make the conversation feel less accusatory and makes talking about safer sex feel much more casual.

The questions you should discuss include (but are not limited to):

- When was your last STI screening and what were you screened for?
- How regularly do you get screened?
- If you're HIV positive, is your viral load undetectable?
- Are you on PrEP?

- Is pregnancy a risk for the kinds of sex you're interested in having? If you don't want to get pregnant, what means of risk mitigation are you using?
- Do either of you have other partners? What methods of risk mitigation do you use with them?

Using language like 'clean' around STI testing can often make people feel judged, especially if they have had an STI or are at an increased risk of contracting one (e.g. if they are a sex worker). Instead, neutral language like 'positive' or 'negative' can be more helpful.

Here are some examples of how to offer this information yourself:

My last STI screening was about a month ago, but I haven't had any new partners in the last three months. I tested negative for HIV, Hep B, chlamydia, gonorrhoea and syphilis, although I'd still rather use barriers.

I'm on PrEP, but I want to use barriers for any kind of sex with a pregnancy risk.

I don't use barriers with my other partner, so we should use them between us.

Remember to be honest about your needs and desires around risk mitigation, and listen to your partner when they bring up theirs. Your partner may need some time to process the feelings brought up by the conversation. Be prepared for vastly different needs and desires around safer sex practices to be a deal breaker.

For example, if you want to use barriers to mitigate the risk of pregnancy but your partner refuses to use them, you're within your right to refuse to have sex with them, or to only want to have other kinds of sex.

You have a right to define your sexual boundaries and have them respected, and you shouldn't feel you have to compromise them unless the compromise is something you're completely comfortable with. If a partner refuses to have a conversation about safer sex practices or refuses to respect your boundaries when it comes to them, you may want to re-assess the situation. Be prepared to take steps for your own wellbeing (mental, physical and emotional) and, depending on how serious the relationship is, be ready to re-evaluate whether it meets those needs.

If you've already had sex, this conversation is just as important, although it may need to take a different form. You'll be asking many of the same questions, but if you've exposed yourself to a risk you're not entirely comfortable with, the focus is now on harm reduction. Depending on what bodies you and your partner have and what kind of sex you had, this may include getting an STI test, buying emergency contraception, or taking PEP. If it is a serious relationship, this is an excellent time to have a conversation about boundaries when it comes to sexual risk, as it reduces the chance you'll be exposed to another risk you're not comfortable with.

Sexually transmitted infections (STIs)

In this section of Chapter 3, we'll go over some of the most common STIs, how they're transmitted and what steps you can take to mitigate the risk of transmission. This isn't an exhaustive list, and some STIs may be more or less common within your communities or geographic locations.

Trans people are at an increased risk of contracting STIs compared with the general population. This is for a number of reasons. The marginalization that trans people experience – such as higher rates of sex work than the general population, higher rates of incarceration, higher rates of homelessness and experiences of discrimination in healthcare – pushes us into situations where we are both more likely to contract an STI and less likely to be able to access adequate care once infected.

There are some risks to be aware of that are specific to trans bodies. For example, testosterone HRT can cause vaginal dryness in some people, making the chance of tissue tearing and risk of STI transmission higher. Post-vaginoplasty people often dilate to stretch vaginal skin, but this can also cause bleeding.

HIV

HIV (human immunodeficiency virus) is a virus that damages the cells in the immune system, leading to a weakened immune system. HIV and AIDS are not the same thing. AIDS (acquired immune deficiency syndrome) is the name given to life-threatening infections that can occur when somebody is HIV positive. Somebody can be HIV positive and not have AIDS.

There is no cure for HIV, but medication (known as antiretroviral medication) now exists that allows for its management. With early detection and treatment, most HIV-positive people will not develop any AIDS-related illnesses or progress to a late-stage HIV infection.

Most people experience mild flu-like symptoms soon after contracting HIV. However, these symptoms may be so mild that somebody may not know they have HIV. This period (known as seroconversion) is when someone with HIV is at their most infectious. However, once seroconversion is over, somebody may not experience any more symptoms for multiple years. Because of this, it's important to get screened for HIV.

HIV can be transmitted through blood, semen, pre-ejaculate fluid, anal mucus, breast milk and vaginal secretions. Ways to mitigate the risk of HIV transmission include using gloves for fingering or fisting, and using dental dams, sterile needles or blades, and condoms. This point about condoms also applies to sex toys or prosthetics. HIV generally does not survive for long outside the body, but can survive for over a month in used needles if the conditions are right.

If you're HIV negative, you may also choose to take PrEP (pre-exposure prophylaxis) medication. If you believe you've been exposed to HIV recently, you can take PEP (post-exposure prophylaxis) medication, although you must take this within 72 hours after you were exposed to HIV. More detailed information on PrEP and PEP is available in the 'Mitigating STI risk' section of this chapter.

HEPATITIS A, B AND C

'Hepatitis' means an inflammation of the liver, and while hepatitis A, B and C are caused by different viruses and are transmitted in slightly different ways, they do have similar symptoms. Sexual activity is not the only way hepatitis can be transmitted. There are other forms of hepatitis – D, E, F and G – but these are generally rare. Vaccines currently exist for hepatitis A and B, but there is currently no vaccine against hepatitis C.

HEPATITIS A

Hepatitis A is transmitted through faecal material. This means an infection may be due to poor hand washing or contaminated food, although some forms of sex also present a transmission risk. These include oral-anal sex ('rimming') and giving oral sex after anal sex. It's also worth noting that using contaminated needles (whether for injection or for piercing play) also presents a transmission risk. Symptoms of hepatitis A may not appear immediately after transmission, but do appear within eight weeks of this point.

Ways to mitigate the risk of hepatitis A transmission include getting the hepatitis A vaccine, using gloves for fingering or fisting, using dental dams for oral-anal sex, using sterile needles or blades and changing condoms between anal and oral sex. This point about condoms also applies to sex toys or prosthetics. If you'd prefer not to use condoms with your toys, sanitizing them between anal and oral sex (see *Chapter 4: Toys and Gear*) or only using them yourself is another option.

Hepatitis A is a short-term illness – in most cases symptoms pass within two months and there are no long-term impacts on health. However, in some cases (1 in every 250 cases) there can be life-threatening complications. Particular groups, such as those with pre-existing liver problems, are more at risk of these complications.

HEPATITIS B

Hepatitis B can be transmitted through blood, semen,

pre-ejaculate fluid and vaginal secretions. This means an infection can result from sharing sex toys, penis-to-vulva or vulva-to-vulva ('scissoring' or 'tribbing') grinding without a barrier, sharing needles or syringes that contain infected blood (whether for injection or for piercing play), oral-anal sex ('rimming'), and oral, vaginal or anal sex without a barrier (including with the sex toys or prosthetics). Hepatitis B can also be transmitted from a pregnant person to their child during pregnancy or birth, or on items like toothbrushes, hair clippers, nail scissors and razors that have been contaminated with traces of infected blood. While hepatitis B is found in trace amounts in saliva, there are no proven cases of it being passed on through kissing. While biting does carry a transmission risk if it breaks skin, infections from bites are rare.

Many people with hepatitis B do not experience any symptoms, and may not ever be aware that they have had the virus. In those who are symptomatic, symptoms generally appear two or three months after exposure.

A vaccine for hepatitis B is available, although you may need a booster injection of the vaccine after five years. Other ways to mitigate the risk of hepatitis B transmission include using barrier methods (including on prosthetics or toys), sanitizing toys between partners, using gloves for fingering or fisting (you may have small cuts on your hands, even if you're unaware of them, and damage to the cuticles is common), using sterile needles or blades and not sharing items like toothbrushes and nail clippers.

Most people are able to fight off a hepatitis B infection in one to three months. However, in some people, an infection may last for six months or more. This is known as 'chronic hepatitis B' and there is a risk it can develop into a life-threatening problem, such as liver cancer.

HEPATITIS C

Hepatitis C is transmitted through blood-to-blood contact. This means an infection can result from sharing unsterilized needles or blades, from sharing notes or straws that are used to snort drugs, or from sharing items like razors or toothbrushes. It can also be transmitted through some kinds of sex. Anal sex (with toys, hands or genitals) and fisting (both vaginal and anal) are particularly risky sex acts, although any sexual activities which have the potential for blood-to-blood contact carry a risk. This includes vaginal sex during menstruation, using large insertable sex toys, rough sex that could cause bleeding, or sharing any BDSM gear that might have blood on it. Sharing 'tub' style pots of lubricant also carries a transmission risk, as the virus can be passed from one person to another on fingers.

There is currently no vaccine for hepatitis C. Steps to mitigate the risk of transmission include wearing gloves for fingering or fisting, using sterile needles or blades, not sharing pots of lube, using condoms on large toys or any kind of toy used for anal play, sterilizing BDSM equipment between partners and using barrier methods during rough sex.

Medication is available to cure hepatitis C, including recently developed tablet-only treatments. However, unlike with other forms of hepatitis, becoming infected with hepatitis C does not grant immunity to it in future. If a hepatitis C infection is left untreated for many years, it can cause scarring of the liver. In severe cases, this may lead to liver cancer or liver failure.

HPV

HPV (human papillomavirus) is an umbrella term for a group of viruses. There are over 100 different strains of HPV and many of them are often inert. Most people will contract a HPV virus at some point in their life, and for many, their body will fight off the infection without medical intervention.

However, some strains (mostly HPV types 6 and 11) can lead to genital warts, and other strains (HPV types 16 and 18) are 'high-risk' types, meaning they can lead to cancers. These include genital cancers like cervical, vaginal or vulva cancer, anal cancer and some kinds of head and neck cancer. Seventy per cent of cervical cancer cases are linked to HPV types 16 and 18, and around 90 per cent of genital warts are linked to HPV types 6 and 11.

A vaccine, known as Gardasil, is available for HPV. This protects against HPV types 6, 11, 16 and 18. In the past, the NHS only made this vaccine available to children assigned female at birth (AFAB) aged 12–13, but this has been extended to all children aged 12–13.

People classed as 'men who have sex with men' who are under the age of 45 are also eligible for the HPV vaccine for free on the NHS – and this includes trans men. Trans women who are seen as having similar risk levels are also eligible for the HPV vaccine for free.

HPV is tested for as part of cervical cancer screenings, which are also known as 'smear tests'. More information on accessing smear tests as a trans person (both as somebody who was AFAB and somebody who has had vaginoplasty) can be found in the 'Getting tested' section of this chapter.

HERPES

There are two kinds of the herpes simplex virus: HSV 1 and HSV 2. While they can both cause genital herpes, HSV 1 is mostly transmitted via oral-to-oral contact. Cold sores are the result of an HSV 1 outbreak. HSV 1 can cause genital herpes through oral sex, but HSV 2 is more associated with genital herpes. A huge number of people have one or both kinds of herpes, and for the most part it is a dermatological problem. The World Health Organization estimates that 3.7 billion people under the age of 50 (67% of the world's population) have HSV 1 and 491 million people between the ages of 15 and 49 (13% of the population) have HSV 2.[8]

Herpes, despite its stigma, is generally a minor issue. In fact, the US Centers for Disease Control and Prevention (CDC) recommends against routine HSV testing because it is expensive and unreliable, and it is usually not included as part of a routine screening.

The symptoms of herpes clear up by themselves, but the blisters can come back – this is known as an outbreak or recurrence. During an outbreak, you can take antiviral medicine, which may help shorten an outbreak by one or two days.

You can contract or transmit herpes even if there are no visible sores. Transmission can occur from skin-to-skin contact, from sharing sex toys, from oral sex, or via fingers. However, herpes cannot be transmitted on items like cups, as the virus dies very quickly when not on the skin. Using gloves and dental dams is a way to mitigate some of the risk of herpes transmission. If you're sharing toys, using condoms on them prevents the transmission of herpes.

GONORRHOEA, CHLAMYDIA AND SYPHILIS
These are bacterial infections that can be passed on through sex.

GONORRHOEA
Gonorrhoea can be present in the throat, anus, vagina or penis. Gonorrhoea in the throat or anus is mostly symptom-free, although some people with gonorrhoea in the rectum may experience discomfort or discharge.

Gonorrhoea can be passed on via oral sex, fingers, anal and vaginal sex or by sharing sex toys. Using external condoms (on both toys and genitals), internal condoms, gloves and dental dams can help mitigate transmission risk. If somebody does contract gonorrhoea, it can be treated with antibiotics. However, there is a strain of gonorrhoea that is resistant to one of the two antibiotics used to treat the infection.

CHLAMYDIA
Chlamydia can also be present in the throat, anus, vagina or penis. Again, in the throat and anus it can be symptom-free, although it may cause discomfort or discharge in the rectum. Cases of chlamydia in post-operative neo-vaginas have been confirmed.[9]

We don't yet know if chlamydia can be spread on fingers. However, we do know that it can be transmitted through anal, vaginal or oral sex, sharing sex toys, or genital-to-genital grinding. Use of barriers like condoms and dental dams mitigates this risk.

SYPHILIS
Syphilis can transmit through anal, oral or vaginal sex, as well

as from sharing sex toys. Untreated syphilis will not go away on its own, and if left to develop can lead to serious issues with the heart, brain or nervous system. In some cases, it can lead to death. However, syphilis can be treated with antibiotics.

Again, use of barriers like dental dams reduces the risk of syphilis transmission, as does using condoms and avoiding sharing sex toys without sanitizing them or using condoms on them.

THREADWORMS AND SHIGELLA

Threadworms aren't strictly an STI, as they can be transmitted on any kind of contaminated surfaces or objects. Threadworms are actually most common in children. However, they and other internal parasites can be transmitted between sex partners, especially in kinds of sex involving anal play. Oral-anal sex is particularly risky, although handling a condom after anal sex can also cause contaminations of the hands, and then possible transmission.

Shigella isn't a parasite, but it is a type of bacteria that transmits in similar ways to parasites, as it's passed on from faecal matter. Some people may experience no symptoms, while others may have diarrhoea or stomach cramps, a fever or vomiting. In some extreme cases, people experience dysentery.

Using a dental dam during oral-anal sex minimizes the risk of parasite transmission. Additionally, washing hands after removing condoms (from both genitals and toys/prosthetics) can help to curb contamination.

Mitigating STI risk

While I've discussed the specific methods of risk mitigation that are suitable for particular STI risks, I also want to discuss these methods in more detail.

VACCINES

Not all STIs have a vaccine, but for those that do, completing a course of vaccination is an excellent way to prevent STI contraction and transmission. If you aren't eligible for a course of vaccinations on a national health service, it may be possible to access them privately. The vaccines for HPV, hepatitis A and hepatitis B are safe for people living with HIV.

USING STERILE NEEDLES

Needle sharing – be it the result of taking hormones, needle play, drug use or at-home tattooing or piercing – carries a significant STI transmission risk. Make sure that you are using sterile needles and you keep injection sites clean by washing your hands, swabbing the injection site with alcohol before injecting, and covering it with a plaster afterwards. Do not share needles with partners, and dispose of needles safely.

While you do not need any kind of prescription to buy a sharps bin, if you're self-medicating with hormones or using needles for piercing play, you may have trouble disposing of a full sharps bin. One option is to hand a full sharps bin to a pharmacy and hope they'll take it, although there is a chance they will refuse. You may want to research needle exchanges within your local area or community, or ask a friend or partner who has a prescription-related sharps bin. Some community centres may also have sharps bins in their bathrooms.

It is worth noting that the needles available from needle exchanges may not be suitable for hormone injections, as these schemes are often aimed at intravenous drug users, while hormones are usually injected with muscular gauge needles. You may need to specifically request needles in the gauge you need, or source your needles elsewhere.

BARRIER METHODS

'Barrier methods' is an umbrella term that refers to any kind of STI risk mitigation that involves placing a layer of latex, nitrile or plastic between bodies. Different barrier methods are useful for different types of sex and combinations of bodies.

GLOVES AND FINGER COTS

Gloves and finger cots are an excellent way to mitigate the risk of skin-to-skin, blood-to-blood or body-fluid-to-blood transmission. Finger cots are also known as 'finger condoms'. Finger cots and gloves are available in both latex and nitrile, so if you have a latex allergy they are still an option for you. While finger cots do reduce wastage, they come with some risks compared to gloves. If a finger cot comes off during use it may be difficult to recover, especially if it's inside the anus.

Gloves also protect your partner from long or sharp nails. If you need extra protection, place cotton balls at the ends of glove fingers, around where your nail would sit. This can also give your nails some protection if fingering or fisting becomes rough. Gloves also reduce friction and hold on to lube better than skin, and reduce the chance of STI transmission through small cuts or damaged cuticles.

Most nitrile and latex gloves are wrist length, so if you're engaging in fisting, you may need longer gloves. Specialist fisting gloves are available, but these may not be disposable. Calving gloves are one option for disposable fisting gloves.

Some gloves may be powdered when they arrive, as this provides extra grip. Make sure to wash this powder off (or buy non-powdered gloves), as this powder causes unnecessary friction and can be an irritant.

DENTAL DAMS

Dental dams are thin squares of latex, polyurethane or nitrile that can be used as a barrier for oral sex. While they're primarily designed for oral-anal or oral-vaginal sex, they can be used as a barrier for other kinds of sex where there's a risk of fluid transmission, like vulva-to-vulva grinding (also known as 'scissoring').

If you're using a dental dam for oral sex, wet the genital or anal area with lube. This will prevent the dam from slipping off. If you're using a latex dental dam, make sure you only use silicone or water-based lubes, as oil-based lubes will damage latex barriers. Do not turn the dam over – only one side should be in contact with your mouth. Some people make sure they remember which side is which by marking one with an 'X'.

Dental dams can be more difficult to find and access than other forms of barrier. If you can't find ready-made dental dams, you can make one yourself, either from a condom (both external or internal) or a glove. To make a dental dam from a condom, unroll it and cut the tip off. Then cut the 'ring' off the bottom of the condom and cut down one side of the condom. If you lay this flat, it will make a rectangle that you can then use as a dental dam.

There are two ways of making a dental dam from a glove. The first creates a square barrier with two fingers, while the other creates one with a thumb. To make a dental dam using the first method, take a glove and cut the middle three fingers off it. Then cut down the middle of the glove from the wrist to where the middle finger used to be. To make one using the second, cut all the fingers off, leaving the thumb, and then slit the glove along the fold line furthest away from the thumb.

INTERNAL CONDOMS

Internal condoms are often called 'female condoms'. However, they can be used both anally and vaginally. Internal condoms are larger and looser than external condoms, and can be inserted up to six hours before sex.

Internal condoms have two rings – a thicker one towards the closed end of the condom and a thinner one towards the open end of the condom. To insert an internal condom, squeeze the side of the condom at the closed end. Then push the thicker ring into the anus or vagina, making sure the thin, outer ring remains outside the body.

Internal condoms work for post-vaginoplasty vaginas, although you may experience difficulty using one depending on the depth of your vagina. They are the safest option for post-metoidioplasty people, especially those who cannot find conventional external condoms that fit them.

EXTERNAL CONDOMS

External condoms are the most well-known form of STI risk

mitigation. They're most often made out of latex, although polyurethane or polyisoprene condoms are available for those with a latex allergy. Condoms made out of lambskin also exist, although they only prevent pregnancy and don't stop the transmission of STIs. Condoms come in many sizes, so make sure that you're using the right size condom for your toy or anatomy.

However, there are other considerations to take into account. If you're using silicone toys (see *Chapter 4: Toys and Gear* for more information on sex toy materials), silicone lube can cause the surface of the toy to deteriorate. Some condoms that come pre-lubed use silicone lubes, so take care you're not using these on toys or prosthetics made of silicone. You may want to specifically seek out lubricated condoms that use water-based lube, or use unlubricated condoms on silicone toys. If you or your partner are post-metoidioplasty, conventional condoms may not fit you. Condoms specially made for small penises may fit you, but if they don't you can use finger cots or the thumbs from latex or nitrile gloves as a condom. Alternatively, the receptive partner can wear an internal condom.

LUBE

While using lube alone doesn't fully mitigate the risk of STI transmission, it can be helpful to use it alongside other mitigation methods. Put simply, friction increases the risk of STI transmission, and lube decreases the friction involved in sex. This is especially important for anal play (as the anus doesn't self-lubricate) or for vaginas that self-lubricate less than others.

People on testosterone HRT have an excess of some bacteria, including some associated with BV (bacterial vaginosis). Because of this, it's good to avoid warming, numbing and flavoured lubes.

More information about lube is available in *Chapter 4: Toys and Gear*.

PrEP and PEP

PrEP and PEP involve some of the same medications, but serve different functions. PrEP – as the name *pre*-exposure prophylaxis suggests – is taken prior to exposure to HIV, while PEP – as suggested by the name *post*-exposure prophylaxis – is taken afterwards.

As a disclaimer, very little work has been done on PrEP and PEP and trans people. The majority of research on PrEP and PEP is done with cisgender gay/bisexual men. While a large international study looking at PrEP called iPrEX[10] did look at the experiences of more than 300 transgender women, it also did not provide many firm conclusions. At the time of writing, no transmasculine people have ever been included in clinical trials of PrEP.

We do know that PrEP and PEP don't interfere with any hormone treatment (with the exception of ethinylestradiol, which is no longer recommended as part of transition). While the iPrEX study didn't draw many firm conclusions about its trans women participants, it did conclude that there was evidence for efficacy. We also know that PrEP is thought to be effective for post-vaginoplasty people. And we know that PrEP doesn't interfere with hormonal birth control.

PREP

The medication used for PrEP is sometimes sold under the brand name Truvada, although generic equivalents do exist and are commonly used in the UK. In the US, a second pill called Descovy has also been approved for PrEP, as has its generic equivalent.

Truvada and its generic equivalent contain two drugs commonly used to treat HIV – tenofovir and emtricitabine. The way that PrEP works is that taking these anti-HIV medications before coming into contact with the virus prevents HIV from establishing infection inside the body.

There are four ways of taking PrEP – daily dosing, on-demand dosing, 'the Ts and Ss', and holiday dosing.

DAILY DOSING

Daily dosing is – as the name suggests – the practice of taking PrEP daily. Taking PrEP every day as directed provides a 99 per cent reduction in HIV risk for HIV-negative people. Some protection is given even if some pills are missed, but the level of risk reduction is reduced – those who take PrEP four times a week have a 96 per cent reduction in risk, while those who only take it two times per week have a 76 per cent reduction in risk.

Vaginal/frontal protection requires daily dosing at least six days a week. Daily dosing is also recommended for those who are the penetrative partner (i.e. the top), including if they are having penis-in-vagina sex and/or are post-phalloplasty. Daily dosing for vaginal and anal sex requires seven days of lead-in time.

ON-DEMAND DOSING

On-demand dosing involves only taking PrEP when needed. However, this kind of dosing is only recommended for receptive anal sex. Studies of on-demand dosing also don't include post-operative genitals, and this style of dosing may also not work as well for those on estradiol.

A double dose (two tablets) needs to be taken at least 2–24 hours before exposure. A second dose (one tablet) should be taken 24 hours after the double dose, and then another dose (one tablet) 24 hours after that. This style of dosing is sometimes known as 2-1-1 dosing as a result.

On-demand PrEP dosing is as effective for tops (those penetrating a partner) as it is for bottoms (those being penetrated). However, as stated above, this kind of dosing has not been studied in post-bottom surgery people, so if you're post-phalloplasty or post-metoidioplasty, daily dosing is recommended instead.

THE TS AND SS/FOUR PILLS PER WEEK

Again, this kind of dosing is only suitable for anal sex. It involves daily dosing for seven days, but then dropping down to four pills per week. These are usually Tuesday, Thursday, Saturday and Sunday, hence the name 'the Ts and Ss'.

People choose to take four pills a week for a number of reasons. They might have sex infrequently, and so not want to take a pill every day. They may be going through a period of sexual inactivity, with the plan to go back to daily dosing in a more sexually active period. Or they may have started with on-demand dosing, but found they took four pills a week more often than not.

HOLIDAY DOSING

This involves taking PrEP around a block of time when you know you'll have a greater risk of exposure to HIV (e.g. you know you'll attend a sex party). It requires seven days of daily dosing before the period, daily dosing during the period, and daily dosing for seven days after the period. The seven days of lead-in mean that this kind of dosing will provide adequate levels of protection for both vaginal and anal sex.

PEP

PEP involves three drugs – again, tenofovir and emtricitabine in the form of Truvada or a generic, although this time in combination with another medication, which is either raltegravir or dolutegravir.

PEP is taken shortly after possible exposure to HIV – preferably within 24 hours but at maximum within 72 hours – and can be used to prevent the HIV virus from taking hold after it has entered the body. It works best if started as soon as possible after exposure. It involves a course of medication for up to four weeks.

In the UK, it is available free on the NHS, but is only provided to those who meet particular guidelines.

If you're given PEP, do not double a dose if you miss one. If you remember a missed dose less than 24 hours after you should take it, take the next dose as soon as possible. If you miss more than 48 hours of PEP, your course will be ended and you will not receive full protection from transmission.

Getting tested

STI SCREENING

The right time to get screened for STIs depends – in part – on your lifestyle. Generally, it's recommended to get tested when:

- you notice any STI symptoms or changes in your body
- you have a new sexual partner
- you and/or your partner(s) have other sexual partners and it's been three to six months since your last test
- you've had sex with somebody who has an STI
- you've had sex without a barrier method or with one that broke.

There are a number of ways of getting tested for STIs, including (but not limited to): sexual health services (sometimes known as GUM clinics), through a GP, or using a home-testing kit. My experiences of getting tested are through NHS-run clinics or home-testing schemes in the UK, so these may not be the same as yours.

Home-testing kits may vary in contents depending on where you live – in some areas of the UK, they may only provide testing for chlamydia, while in others they may also offer gonorrhoea, HIV and syphilis testing.

It's important to note that there's a 'window' between contracting an STI and when it'll show in a test, and this varies for different STIs. For chlamydia and gonorrhoea, it's up to two weeks, while for HIV it's up to either 45 or 90 weeks (depending on the kind of test), and for syphilis it's 12 weeks.

Most NHS sexual health clinics offer a drop-in service if you're just there for a check-up. You'll be asked for a name and contact details, so that your results can be passed on to you. The name you provide does not have to be your real name, and information on your results will not be passed to your GP without your consent. A doctor or nurse will ask you questions on your sexual behaviour and partners, using this to inform what tests they'll offer you.

Healthcare providers may have little or no experience with trans patients, and/or may come to the appointment with assumptions about what your body looks like and what kind of sex you have, which may not reflect your actual sexual behaviour at all. For example, they may assume that trans men have sex predominantly or exclusively with cisgender women, so are at minimal risk of contracting HIV. While some trans men do have sex with cisgender women, this assumption means that other sexual behaviours and needs when it comes to sexual healthcare go unaddressed – a US-based study found that 28 per cent of the trans men who have sex with men that they recruited for their study had *never* had a HIV test!"

If you find self-advocacy difficult, you may want to take an advocate with you – local trans organizations and groups may be able to put you in contact with or provide you with an advocate. Pressing may feel awkward, but you deserve to get the healthcare you need. If you live in a town or city with a large LGBT+ district, healthcare workers at sexual health clinics based there may have more experience with trans patients.

Depending on your anatomy and sexual behaviour, you may be offered tests that include:

- a vaginal swab
- an oral swab
- an anal swab
- a blood sample
- a urine sample.

If you have dysphoria around your genitals being touched or seen, it's worth asking if you can self-administer some of the swabs. In some clinics, all swabs are self-administered.

The results of some tests are same-day, while others may take up to two weeks. You can let the clinic know how you'd like to receive your results when you give them your contact details – options may include by text, by phone call, or by post in an unmarked letter. If any of your tests are positive, the clinic will ask you to come back to discuss your results and any treatment you might need.

WHAT IF I TEST POSITIVE?

If you test positive for any STI, the clinic will want to make an appointment with you to discuss next steps. You should let your partner(s) know that you tested positive – some clinics will do this for you anonymously, if you would find the conversation too awkward – so that they can get tested and (if necessary) start treatment.

If you do test positive for an STI, remember that this does not reflect your value or worth. You are not dirty for having contracted an STI any more than somebody contracting a cold is dirty. You are not wrong or a bad person for having an STI. In most cases, STIs are treatable, and contracting one is not the end of your life or sex life.

Pregnancy

In this section, we'll talk about the impact that different aspects of medical transition have on fertility. We'll also talk about what birth control and emergency contraception options are available to people on testosterone HRT, as well as forms of birth control that can be used to suppress menstruation. Additionally, we'll discuss accessing abortion services for transmasculine people, and what some of the hurdles in doing so may be.

MEDICAL TRANSITION AND FERTILITY

As mentioned in *Chapter 2: Anatomy and Bodies*, different aspects of medical transition can have an impact on fertility. This includes both surgical and non-surgical medical procedures, such as orchiectomy (removal of the testes), hysterectomy (removal of the uterus), oophorectomy (removal of ovaries), taking oestrogen and anti-androgens, taking testosterone, or taking gonadotrophin releasing hormone (GnRH) analogues (sometimes known as puberty blockers, although they are also used in the treatment of trans adults).

The pubertal suppression that GnRH analogues offer is reversible. For example, if an AFAB person discontinued puberty blockers without starting testosterone, their period would return within a period of approximately one year,[12] even following long-term use. GnRH analogues cannot be relied on for contraceptive protection.

Testosterone generally causes periods to cease within six months of starting HRT, which does make conceiving more difficult, and if you're trying to conceive, it's recommended you stop taking testosterone.

However, there isn't a direct correlation between being able to get pregnant and being able to menstruate – in a 2014 study[13] of trans men who became pregnant, several participants were able to become pregnant before their periods returned, and one third of pregnancies in the study were unplanned. Testosterone HRT shouldn't and can't be relied on as birth control – if you're on testosterone, still have a uterus and are engaging in kinds of sex with a pregnancy risk, make sure you have another kind of birth control in place, such as oral contraception, or condoms.

Taking oestrogen has impacts on sperm production, affecting the quantity and quality of sperm produced, as well as sometimes the ability to produce sperm at all. In some cases, coming off oestrogen for a few months means a person can produce sperm again, although medical assistance – such as in vitro fertilization (IVF) – may still be needed to achieve a pregnancy.

However, the impact of HRT on fertility varies from person to person. While the risk of accidental pregnancy is low, it's not zero. As with testosterone, oestrogen and anti-androgens should not be relied on for contraception.

Any surgical procedure that removes the gonads – that is, the organs that produce either sperm or egg cells – will cause infertility. This includes orchiectomy (removal of the testes), as well as vaginoplasty/vulvoplasty (creation of a vagina and/or vulva).

However, not all bottom surgery options will remove the gonads – metoidioplasty and phalloplasty can be performed without the removal of the vagina, uterus or ovaries. If your ovaries are still intact, you still have the risk/potential of becoming pregnant.

It is worth noting that trans people's reproductive capacities have been and still are restricted in many ways across the globe. Lawmakers may require sterilization as a condition of legal gender recognition, either indirectly (by mandating surgeries where sterility is an outcome) or explicitly (by mandating 'surgically irreversible infertility').

CONTRACEPTION FOR PEOPLE ON TESTOSTERONE

If testosterone alone doesn't work as birth control, what can people on testosterone use as contraception? The good news is that all the contraception available to cis women can also be used to prevent pregnancy by those on testosterone. However, this is with some caveats. Even different cisgender women have a different 'right' contraception for their bodies and needs, and not every form of birth control will suit you as an individual. Additionally, combining birth control with HRT may impact the dose required for HRT. This is especially the case for oestrogen-based or combined hormonal contraceptive methods. While you *can* use these methods, make sure your doctor is aware of and knowledgeable about both birth control and HRT.

If you don't have access to a knowledgeable doctor, or you don't want to impact your HRT, or the idea of oestrogen-based contraception is uncomfortable for you, you still have access to progesterone-only or non-hormonal methods. The following tables give an overview of some of these options. Do note that none of them protect against STIs.

Progesterone-only contraception methods

Method	Description	Positives	Negatives
Progesterone-only pill (sometimes called the POP, or 'mini pill')	Oral pill. Taken daily, around the same time every day.	99% effective if taken correctly.	Can be made less effective by some medicines and certain types of antibiotic. Can cause side effects in the first few months, such as breast tenderness.
IUS (intrauterine system)	A small plastic device shaped like a T, placed in the uterus through the vagina. Can last 3–5 years, depending on the brand.	99% effective. Lasts for 3–5 years. Not impacted by other medication, vomiting or diarrhoea.	Has to be inserted via the vagina, which some may find triggers their dysphoria. Small risk of infection after the IUS has been implanted. Small risk of the IUS being displaced.
Contraceptive implant	A flexible plastic rod implanted in the upper arm just under the skin, under local anaesthetic. Lasts up to 3 years.	99% effective. Lasts for 3 years. Not impacted by other medication, vomiting or diarrhoea.	Temporary side effects in the first few months, such as headaches. Can cause or make acne worse.
Contraceptive injection	An injection containing progesterone. Effective for 8, 12 or 13 weeks, depending on form used.	Over 99% effective. Not impacted by antibiotics, vomiting or diarrhoea. Self-injection with Sayana Press form may mean only one annual clinic visit.	Can cause acne. Can't be removed, unlike an implant. Can reduce bone mineral density. Can cause weight gain, headaches, mood swings or breast tenderness.

Non-hormonal contraception methods

Method	Description	Positives	Negatives
Copper IUD (intrauterine device)	A T-shaped plastic device containing copper, placed in the uterus through the vagina. Once fitted, the IUD can last 5–10 years.	99% effective. Can be used as emergency contraception. Effective immediately. Not impacted by antibiotics, vomiting or other medication – can be used in combination with other contraception.	Has to be inserted via the vagina, which some may find triggers their dysphoria. Small risk of infection after the IUD has been implanted. Small risk of the IUD being displaced or pushed out.
Diaphragms and cervical caps	Silicone devices inserted into the vagina to cover the cervix, preventing sperm from entering the uterus. Must be used with a spermicide – a gel that contains chemicals that kill sperm cells. They are placed in the vagina before sex (although more spermicide will need to be added if this is more than 3 hours before sex).	Not impacted by any medications taken in tablet form, or vomiting.	High real-life failure rate, as most people do not follow directions precisely – the failure rate for cervical caps is 14% in those who haven't given birth and 29% in those who have. Some people are sensitive to spermicide. May cause cystitis (a bladder infection). Must be left in after sex for at least 6 hours.

EMERGENCY CONTRACEPTION

If you've had sex without a method of contraception or when your method of contraception has failed (e.g. a condom has broken), you may want to seek out emergency contraception.

Emergency contraception and abortion aren't the same thing – abortion ends a pregnancy, while emergency contraception prevents a pregnancy.

All of the contraception methods we've discussed so far (with the exception of the copper IUD) don't function as emergency contraception. What should a person on testosterone do if they need emergency contraception?

Both forms of emergency contraceptive pill are progesterone based, and so will work for those on testosterone. The two kinds of emergency contraception pill are levonorgestrel and ulipristal acetate, although they're known by different brand names.

An IUD must be fitted by a trained doctor or nurse – your GP may be able to fit one, or you can specifically seek out a sexual health clinic. In order to prevent pregnancy as emergency contraception, it must be fitted within 120 hours (five days) of unprotected sex.

If you're 16 or older, you can buy the levonorgestrel pill from most pharmacies, and some will stock the ulipristal acetate pill as well. However, UK pharmacies have a policy to only provide contraception to the individual who is going to use it. If you're read as a cisgender man, they may refuse to provide you with emergency contraception unless you disclose your trans status.

CONTRACEPTION FOR MENSTRUATION SUPPRESSION

Some methods of contraception can impact the frequency of periods. If you find having a period makes you dysphoric, you might want to use birth control to stop them.

Do note that different bodies behave differently and what works for suppressing or preventing periods in one person may not work for another. In some cases, contraception might make your periods heavier or longer. There's no guarantee what impact contraception will have on your periods, and you may experience 'breakthrough bleeding' randomly.

While it's generally safe to skip your period using contraception, it's worth consulting with a trans-friendly doctor beforehand.

Contraception that can impact menstruation

Method	Possible impact on menstruation	Suitable for those on T?
IUS (intrauterine system)	May cause periods to be lighter or shorter, or may cause them to stop completely. Can cause irregular bleeding at first.	Yes
Contraceptive injection	May reduce heavy periods and period pain. Can cause periods to stop completely. May cause periods to become irregular, heavier or longer.	Yes
Progesterone-only pill (sometimes called the POP, or 'mini pill')	Can cause periods to become irregular. They may stop altogether, happen less often, become lighter or happen more often. May cause 'spotting' between periods.	Yes
Contraceptive implant	Periods may become irregular or stop altogether.	Yes

Abortion

Abortion is the process of ending a pregnancy that has already begun. It's more common than you might think: one in three cisgender women in the UK will have an abortion by the age of 45.

If you live in England, Scotland or Wales, you are entitled to an abortion payed for by the NHS. This is also the case if you're a UK citizen from Northern Ireland travelling to England for an abortion. While sexual health services or your GP cannot carry out an abortion, they can refer you to an abortion service. You can also self-refer to abortion services in some parts of the UK.

For some people, the decision to have an abortion may be very difficult, while for others it may be very easy. There is no wrong way to feel about having an abortion, and each person is different.

There are two ways of ending unwanted pregnancies – medical abortions and surgical abortions. Which type you can have depends on a variety of factors (such as how far the pregnancy has progressed), but you should always be allowed to choose which kind of abortion you would prefer, as long as it suits your medical needs.

A medical abortion is also sometimes known as 'the abortion pill'. It can be performed up to 24 weeks of pregnancy, but it may be difficult to access or only available as an inpatient past ten weeks, depending on where you live. Having a medical abortion involves taking two medications called mifepristone and misoprostol. Mifepristone ends a pregnancy, while misoprostol expels it from the body through cramping and bleeding. When and where you take the two pills depends on your country and/or state's laws, as well as the particular rules of your clinic.

The most common form of surgical abortion is 'vacuum aspiration'. This procedure can be used until 15 weeks of pregnancy, takes place under general or local anaesthetic, takes around five to ten minutes, and does not require stitches. In this procedure, suction is used to remove a pregnancy through the cervix.

Recovery for vacuum aspiration abortion is normally around an hour, and most patients go home on the same day.

If a pregnancy has progressed past 15 weeks, a different surgical method known as surgical dilation and evacuation may be carried out. This procedure normally takes place under general anaesthetic and takes around 10–20 minutes. After a surgical dilation and evacuation abortion, you may need to stay overnight in the hospital, and you may bleed for up to three weeks after having an abortion.

Some factors trans people have cited as impacting their decision to choose medical abortion over surgical abortion include wanting a method that feels 'least invasive', feels 'most private' or 'does not require anaesthesia', or wanting to avoid interactions with medical providers where they might be misgendered. Others have stated that they choose surgical over medical abortion due to it taking the shortest amount of time, it being less painful, and wanting to avoid passing a pregnancy at home.[14]

ACCESSING ABORTION WHEN TRANSMASCULINE

Abortion access is often treated as an issue relevant only to cisgender women. This isn't true, however, and transmasculine people are not only impacted by abortion restrictions, but also experience barriers to accessing abortion beyond those of cisgender women, due to medical transphobia and cissexism. While exact figures aren't available, it's estimated that between 462 and 530 trans people were abortion patients in the US in 2017,[15] although this statistic is likely to be below the actual number, as many healthcare providers don't collect data on their patients' trans status.

I'd love to be able to say that there's an easy way to navigate transphobic barriers to abortion, but the reality is there isn't. There is no healthcare organization that is completely devoid of casual cissexism or transphobia. Even if there was, pointing to individual organizations as the solution means assuming that all trans people have the luxury of choice. This isn't the case, particularly for trans people who live in rural or remote areas, or have difficulty accessing transport.

The most obvious issue for those accessing abortion while trans is transphobia from medical professionals. At its most extreme, this may mean a medical professional refusing to give care to somebody because of their transgender status. In 2017, Stonewall's *LGBT in Britain – Trans Report*[16] found that 7 per cent of their trans respondents had been refused healthcare because of their trans status. Even when healthcare isn't denied outright to trans people, we may be misgendered or harassed by medical staff.

As with accessing STI testing, you may want to take a health-care advocate with you. Depending on your location, local trans organizations and groups may be able to put you in contact with or provide you with an advocate.

Erectile dysfunction medication

Some people find that anti-androgens can make it harder to gain or maintain an erection (see *Chapter 2: Anatomy and Bodies*). While this may be a positive change for some (or one they're ambivalent about), other people may choose to take medication for erectile dysfunction. Prescription ED (erectile dysfunction) medications like Viagra, Cialis and Levitra do not interact with

HRT, meaning they are just as safe and effective for those on HRT as those off it. However, while these medications make erections easier to gain and maintain, they do still require their user to be aroused to work.

Prescribed ED medications are generally quite safe, although they may not be suitable for those with some health conditions, such as low blood pressure, those taking some other medications, and those who have recently had a heart attack or stroke.

Combining ED medication and poppers is extremely dangerous. 'Poppers' is an umbrella term for many different alkyl nitrite drugs. Sold in small bottles, they're usually a liquid that produces a vapour that is then inhaled. Because it's illegal to advertise them for human consumption, they're often sold as 'leather cleaners', 'room odourisers' or 'VHS cleaners'. Both poppers and Viagra, for example, cause a blood pressure drop. The combination of the two can result in fainting, strokes or heart attacks. There's no really clear guidance on how long a person should wait between taking Viagra and doing poppers to reduce this risk, although some people recommend waiting 24 hours between using the two.

CHAPTER 4

Toys and Gear

In this chapter, we'll discuss sex toys, lube and some other kinds of gear that you might use during sex (although if you're looking for information on kink/BDSM gear, *Chapter 9: Kink* may be more useful).

We'll talk about:

- what sex toys and lube are
- some of the most common myths around sex toys and lube
- sex toy material and lube ingredient safety
- the different kinds of sex toys that are available
- adapting toys for different bodies.

Sex toys 101

Put simply, sex toys are objects used during sex (solo or partnered) in order to increase pleasure. There are many names for these kinds of objects – pleasure products, marital aids, sexual aids – but I personally prefer the term 'sex toy', as I love the idea of sex as something playful. I do understand why some people dislike it, especially if they associate 'play' or 'toy' with children, but that's not an association my brain makes. While I'll use that terminology throughout this chapter, if you dislike it, feel free to cross it out and replace it with another term you like!

Sex toys have existed throughout human history. In my past life as an archaeologist, I remember giggling through a lecture that mentioned 'olisbokollikes', an Ancient Greek term for dildos made out of bread. While we're unsure if olisbokollikes actually existed or if they were just a joke about the shape of a loaf of bread, the existence of the term means we know that sex toys have existed for thousands of years.

Modern sex toys are somewhat different from their ancient counterparts. Electricity has made powered vibrators possible, and the creation of silicone dildos by the disability rights activist Gosnell Duncan in the early 1970s has made non-porous and body-safe materials more prevalent.

Sex toys come in a wide variety of forms and functions, from non-penetrative rideable vibrators and penis extenders for post-metoidioplasty people to butt plugs and nipple toys. The 'Types of sex toys' section of this chapter gives a more complete overview of the kinds of sex toys that are available.

Why do people use sex toys?

There's almost as many reasons that people use sex toys as there are people. For some, sex toys may be the only way that they can orgasm or the easiest way that they can orgasm. Others may enjoy the different sensations that sex toys can provide. For some transgender people, using sex toys can also relieve gender dysphoria or feel affirming.

Sex toy safety

Currently, there are no specific regulations on sex toys in the UK. While this doesn't mean there's no regulation at all on the sex toy market – toys still have to pass electronics safety checks, for example – it does mean that some toxic or non-body safe toys are still widely available.

Sex toys are also largely unregulated within the US, with the Food and Drug Administration only regulating devices that are intended to treat 'sexual dysfunction' in a medical or therapeutic context. While not all toys labelled as 'novelty use' are unsafe, this label does allow some sex toys to make it to market despite containing materials banned in other products, such as children's toys.

When thinking about sex toy safety, there are generally two areas to consider: toxic toys and toys that are porous.

TOXIC TOYS

Some toys made from 'jelly rubber' or polyvinyl chloride (PVC) are produced using phthalates, which are used to make these materials soft and flexible. When introduced to the body – through the mucous membranes of the vagina, mouth or anus – phthalates can cause a number of health issues, such as endocrine disruption.

However, a toy being marked as 'phthalate-free' doesn't necessarily mean that it's non-toxic. For example, a PVC toy may contain chlorine, an irritant which can cause skin burning or a skin rash, even if it's phthalate-free.

POROUS TOYS

Porosity is another thing to consider when choosing a sex toy. Materials with large pores – such as thermoplastic elastomers and thermoplastic rubbers (TPE and TPR) – can harbour bacteria, mildew and fungi, and cannot be properly sanitized. This means that even after cleaning, a used porous toy carries the risk of introducing bacteria or fungus to the body – in some cases, porous toys can reintroduce yeast infections if they were used during an infection.

One caveat is that it can be difficult to find sleeve-style toys (see the 'Types of sex toys' section of this chapter if you're unsure what that means) that are made from non-porous materials, especially at an affordable price. Additionally, a non-insertable toy carries less risk of infection than those that are inserted into the body, as it won't come into contact with the delicate mucous membranes of the anus or vagina. However, I would still recommend keeping a close eye on any porous toys, and disposing of them at the sight of any discolouration or odd smells.

A quick guide to common sex toy materials

Material	Description	Risk of toxicity?	Porous?
Silicone	Functionally non-porous, odourless and easy to clean. Can vary in firmness, from squishy to soft.	No	No
Glass	Body safe, but be sure to check for chips and cracks before each use.	No	No

Steel and aluminium	Body safe and compatible with all lubricant types.	No	No
ABS (acrylonitrile butadiene styrene) plastic	A very firm plastic, commonly used in vibrators.	No	No
TPE/TPR	Sometimes called 'skin safe rubber'. These toys also shouldn't be stored touching other toys, as the material may break down.	No	Yes (Medical grade TPE is functionally non-porous. However, few sex toys are made from it.)
'Jelly' rubber	An unstable – but cheap to produce – material. Semi-transparent, often flexible.	Yes	Yes
PVC	Another cheap material.	Yes	Yes
Latex	Latex in sex toys isn't regulated by the US in the way it is in condoms, so may contain phthalates.	Yes	Yes

Of course, these aren't the only factors to consider in using sex toys safely. Safe design is also important – any toy used anally needs to have a wide, flared base to prevent it from being lost or stuck – as is cleaning toys regularly and well.

Cleaning sex toys

Cleaning your sex toys is an important step in using them – uncleaned sex toys can transmit STIs from person to person.[17] How you need to clean your sex toy depends on the material it's made of, as well as whether it has a motor or not.

A basic way to clean non-porous sex toys is to use simple

soap and warm water. While you can buy 'sex toy cleaners', these are often simply just soap in a bottle, and a scent-free antibacterial soap that isn't marketed specifically for sex toy use will work just as well. If you can't submerge your toy because it has a motor and isn't waterproof, you can still clean it with soap, and then wipe it clean with a damp cloth.

Non-motorized sex toys can be cleaned more deeply through a number of methods. One way of deep cleaning is to submerge the toy in boiling water for eight to ten minutes. Alternatively, if you have a dishwasher with a 'sanitize' setting, this can be used to clean your toys.

Once your toy is clean, either leave it to air dry or dry it off completely with a clean towel before putting it away in storage.

Myths about sex toys

Despite sex toys being thousands of years old, there are still plenty of misconceptions and misinformation around them. When I worked in a sex shop doing customer service, I heard almost no end of them! These myths come from a variety of sources, but the reason so many of them prevail is due to the stigma around sex toys that prevents open communication. While I can't bust every myth around sex toys in this section, I've covered some of the most common myths that persist to this day.

MYTH 1: SEX TOYS ARE A REPLACEMENT FOR PARTNERS

This is one of the most ubiquitous myths about sex toys, and it can present in a number of ways. One example is the idea that sex toys are owned by single people who aren't having partnered sex. Another is the flip-side of that – the idea that couples who use sex toys are doing so because the flame has gone out in their relationship. While it's less common, I have seen a variation of this myth pop up in transmasculine spaces, where pre-/non-bottom surgery people who top using toys or prosthetics feel that they're replaceable by the toy they're using on their partner/s.

All of these variations stem from something that isn't true. A sex toy is not a partner, it is a tool. Sex toys are used by people in all kinds of relationship statuses, both solo and partnered.

MYTH 2: SEX TOYS ARE GUARANTEED TO CAUSE ORGASMS
Just as an orgasm isn't guaranteed from any other source, there's no guarantee that a sex toy will cause somebody to have an orgasm. If you can't orgasm with a sex toy, there is nothing wrong or broken about you.

This may be for situational reasons – just as somebody might not be 'in the mood' for other kinds of sex – or it may be because of anatomical reasons.

Not all genitals are shaped the same, and sex toys that work for one particular person's anatomy may not work for another. Rabbit vibrators are an excellent example of this – there are more variables on a rabbit vibrator than a single use vibrator, and if either the shaft or clitoral stimulator don't fit your body, you might find it difficult or impossible to orgasm.

MYTH 3: SILICONE SEX TOYS WILL
'MELT' IF STORED TOGETHER
This myth is really prevalent – even in sex positive spaces – and it's not true! But there are two main reasons why it's still believed by so many people. The first is that while silicone toys won't

cause each other to 'melt' through touch, jelly toys will. Because the sex toy industry has been unregulated for so long, in the past it was exceptionally common (and still is, especially on wholesale websites) to see toys sold as 'silicone' (or 'silicon') when they were jelly, TPE,or some other kind of porous or toxic material.

The second reason is that, in most cases (there are exceptions for specific manufacturers' lubes and dildo silicones), silicone lube *does* cause damage to silicone toys.

Lube 101

Put simply, lube is a gel or liquid used during sex (partnered or solo) that's used to reduce friction. Lube is essential to anal sex, as anuses do not self-lubricate, but is also valuable in all kinds of sex, including solo play, vaginal sex, oral sex, hand to genital contact or genital to genital contact (sometimes called 'scissoring' or 'frottage').

While I've touched on one reason somebody might want to use lube – anal sex – there are many other possibilities. A person on testosterone might find they don't self-lubricate as much as they'd like to, for example.

Remember, every person's body is different, and a lube that works for someone else might not work for you.

TYPES OF LUBE

There are four general categories of lube: water, oil, silicone and 'hybrid', each of which functions slightly differently and has its own compatibilities and incompatibilities. There are also other kinds of lube, such as flavoured and warming lubes.

While compatibility isn't the only thing you should think about when choosing a lube (see the 'Lube ingredients to watch out for' section), making sure the lube you choose is compatible with the way you want to use it is vital.

WATER-BASED LUBES

Water-based lubes are very varied, coming in a variety of textures, thicknesses and consistencies. Water-based lubes 'dry up' during use, as the water in them is absorbed into the body, but they can be 'reactivated' by the application of water or more lube. Thicker and more 'gel'-like water-based lubes tend to last longer than other kinds of water-based lubes.

Water-based lubes are compatible with silicone toys and condoms. However, some water-based lubes with thinner consistencies may not be suitable for anal sex. In addition, water-based lubes aren't usable for shower or water-based sex and may require reapplication more frequently than other kinds of lube.

OIL-BASED LUBES

Oil-based lubes are the most ancient kind – there's evidence of oils being used as a lubricant as far back as 800 BCE – and they're still used in the present day. Some people use natural oils – like coconut oil – while others use specially created lubes that are oil based.

Oil-based lubes are longer lasting than water-based lubes, and can have a dual use as massage oil. However, they also cause latex to degrade, meaning they're not compatible with latex condoms, dental dams or gloves. They can be used with non-latex barriers, such as polyurethane condoms or nitrile gloves.

Oil-based lubricants are more difficult to clean up than

water-based lubes and may stain sheets. Additionally, not all oils or oil-based lubricants are made equal! Coconut oil, for example, has a very high pH, making it alkaline. Because the pH of the vagina is naturally acidic, using coconut oil as lube for vaginal use can disrupt this natural pH, sometimes leading to vaginal infection.

SILICONE-BASED LUBES

Silicone lubes are longer lasting than water-based lubes and don't require frequent reapplication. They're compatible with condoms and, unlike water-based lube, can also be used for shower or water sex.

However, silicone lubes can cause silicone toys to degrade. Silicone lubes are also harder to clean off than water-based lubes and may cause staining to upholstery or fabrics.

Something to note is that many lubricated condoms use silicone lube. If you're planning on using condoms on a toy, it's worth taking the time to check if the lube on the condoms is water based, or deciding to use unlubricated condoms and lube them yourself.

HYBRID LUBES

Hybrid lubes are a mix of water- and silicone-based lubes. In most cases, they're predominantly water based, with a small amount of silicone lube added to reduce the need for reapplication and increase the viscosity of the lube. As hybrid lubes are newer to the market, less research on them exists.

Hybrid lubes are compatible with condoms. However, as the silicone content of hybrid lubes varies, different hybrid lubes may have different levels of compatibility with different toys.

One way to test if your lube is compatible with your toy is to do a 'patch test', leaving a drop of lube on the base of your toy – or any other part that isn't used – and seeing if the silicone surface shows signs of degradation.

FLAVOURED LUBES

Flavoured lubes are primarily marketed for oral sex and are available in a wide variety of flavours. However, if you're using them on vulvas or in conjunction with vaginal sex or penetration, be cautious and look for a lube that is sugar- or glycerin-free (see 'Lube ingredients to watch out for' below).

WARMING LUBES

Warming lubes – as the name suggests – induce a warm or hot sensation when used, although the lube itself is still cold. Some people complain about stinging, irritation and redness after using warming lubes, and most sensation lubricants contain glycerin, so be sure to check the ingredient list.

NUMBING LUBES

Lubes that numb pain are frequently marketed as making sex – especially anal sex – 'easier'. Numbing lubes often contain benzocaine – an ingredient that should be avoided – and I wouldn't recommend them at all. Pain is the body's way of indicating that something is wrong, and when it comes to sex, having no feedback from your body can lead to injuries, such as microtears to delicate anal tissue.

Quick reference to lube compatibility

Lube type	Safe for use with…?				
	Vaginal use	Anal use	Silicone toys	Glass/metal/ABS plastic toys	Latex barriers
Water	Yes	Yes	Yes	Yes	Yes
Oil	Sometimes – some oils like coconut oil have an alkaline pH, disrupting the natural acidic pH of the vagina.	Yes	Yes	Yes	No
Silicone	Yes	Yes	No	Yes	Yes
Hybrid	Yes	Yes	Some-times – do a patch test first.	Yes	Yes

LUBE INGREDIENTS TO WATCH OUT FOR

Not all lubes are made equal, and plenty contain ingredients that may cause irritation or infection in some people. This section isn't a complete list of ingredients to avoid, but does highlight some of the most common problematic ingredients. While these ingredients are not guaranteed to cause problems and you or somebody you know may have used a lube containing them with no issues, there is scientific evidence suggesting they are to be avoided.

GLYCERIN

Glycerin is a super common ingredient in lubes, especially ones that are flavoured or warming. It's a sugar alcohol and tends to be used in water-based lubes to make them longer lasting, although it's also used as a sweetener in some flavoured lubes. Glycerin in the vagina can lead to an overgrowth of yeast, and from there vaginal yeast infections, especially in people more prone to these.

PETROLATUM OR PETROLEUM JELLY

Petroleum-based products – such as Vaseline – also cause problems with pH, contributing to bacterial overgrowth and potential bacterial vaginosis.[18]

NONOXYNOL-9

Nonoxynol-9 is an ingredient in a lot of spermicides. While it does kill sperm, it also kills natural vaginal bacteria.[19] The imbalance of vaginal bacteria can lead to infections like bacterial vaginosis. Additionally, some people find that nonoxynol-9 causes them to experience uncomfortable inflammation and irritation.

BENZOCAINE OR LIDOCAINE

These ingredients are found in 'numbing' lubes, which I wouldn't recommend in general. In addition, benzocaine can produce allergic contact dermatitis.[20]

Types of sex toys

Earlier in this chapter I covered safety when it comes to sex toys, but not what kind of sex toys are available. This section is a broad overview – I don't name specific brands or products (especially given that the sex toy market is forever changing), but rather give some broad categories and some of the variations you can find within them. I'm also not discussing toys for bondage or other kinds of BDSM activities in this chapter – see *Chapter 9: Kink* for more information.

Remember that sex toys do not have to be used in the way that they're designed for (with the exception of making sure that anal toys have a solid flared base!). A toy that's intended for clitoral or g-spot stimulation could be used on nipples or a penis, for example. If a toy has no mention of your ideal use in its marketing or packaging copy, it doesn't mean you can't use it that way!

DILDOS

Dildos are sex toys intended for insertion. They vary in shape and size, including in how much they resemble a penis, and generally they don't vibrate. Dildos can be used on their own, with other toys (a vibrating cock ring can turn a dildo into a vibrator), or worn in a harness and used for partnered penetrative sex. Dildos can be used both vaginally and anally, and some are curved to hit the prostate or g-spot. For a dildo to be safe for anal use, it should have a flared base – one larger than the widest point on the dildo. A flared base also means that a dildo is wearable in a harness.

Some dildos are called 'pack and play', meaning that they can be used for penetrative sex, but also for packing (see *Chapter 2: Anatomy and Bodies*), and create a noticeable bulge on the wearer under clothes. Some products are also usable for standing to pee, and may be called '3-in-1' ('4-in-one' if they include a sleeve device) pack and plays, or prosthetics. Some trans people really dislike calling these products anything but prosthetics, so in the rest of this book I'll refer to both strap-ons and prosthetics when it comes to sex using them.

Double-ended dildos come in various shapes and can be used for mutual penetration between partners or for double penetration of the same person, depending on the shape. Some double-ended dildos are sold as 'strapless strap-ons', with a bulb-shaped end for the wearer and a longer end for penetrating their partner. However, these toys require Kegel strength to hold in place, and are often more difficult to use than conventional strap-ons, especially when it comes to using them for anal sex.

VIBRATORS

Vibrators are – in the broadest terms – toys that vibrate/move continuously to create stimulation or sensation. Most vibrators in the modern day are electric, although hand-cranked vibrators did exist in the past!

Some people describe the sensation of vibrators as 'rumbly' or 'buzzy', which isn't a description of the strength of a vibrator. These generally refer to slightly different sensations, the former referring to vibrations that feel 'high pitched' and are felt on the surface level of the body, while the former refers to 'lower pitched' vibrations that are felt more deeply. Different people have different preferences when it comes to kinds of vibration – I personally have a strong preference for rumbly vibrations, but other people may find them overstimulating and uncomfortable or painful.

Vibrators can be made with particular anatomies in mind – such as vaginas or prostates – but many made for external stimulation can be utilized in anatomy-neutral ways.

WAND

A wand vibrator – think of the classic 'personal massager' shape – consists of a handle that's attached to a round vibrating head. While battery-powered wand vibrators do exist, they're more often mains-powered or rechargeable. This means they can be more on the powerful and rumbly end of vibrators. Wands aren't intended for internal use, but there are attachments available that will allow you to use a wand internally.

The broad head of this style of vibrator means it can be used on all shapes and sizes of genitals – including between bodies – and it can be used on penises without the need to maintain an erection. The deeper, rumblier vibrations that mains-powered wands offer can aid in stimulating embedded erectile tissue for those post-phalloplasty, as well as allowing these wands to be used over clothes for those who have issues with dysphoria during sex.

BULLET

Some – but not all – bullet-style vibrators do resemble their namesake. In more general terms, a bullet vibrator is a small vibrator with a small surface area that's primarily intended for clitoral stimulation.

However, they can be used in plenty of other ways. Their small size means they can be used for muffing (see *Chapter 5: Manual Sex and Grinding*) and can fit easily between partners' bodies during penetrative sex. Bullet vibrators can also be used to stimulate nipples, penises (including post-op penises), and the perineum, among other parts of the body.

G-SPOT

G-spot vibrators are designed to be used internally to stimulate the g-spot (see *Chapter 2: Anatomy and Bodies*). Vibrators specifically intended for g-spot stimulation are distinguished from other internal vibrators by a curved shape and a large, sometimes bulbous head. If a g-spot vibrator has a flared base, it can also be used for prostate stimulation.

While g-spot vibrators tend to be quite long, you may not need the whole toy to reach the g-spot – on average, it's only 1–2 inches inside the vagina. Every person's body is different, though, so yours may be more or less deep than average.

DUAL STIMULATION/'RABBIT'

Dual stimulation vibrators are designed for simultaneous clitoral and vaginal stimulation. They're sometimes called rabbit vibrators due to the fact that the first model to become widely popular had a 'rabbit ear'-shaped clitoral stimulator. For some people, dual stimulation vibrations can lead to 'blended orgasms', where they experience both a clitoral and vaginal orgasm at the same time.

It is worth noting that dual stimulation vibrators are often very anatomy specific. You may not enjoy using a dual stimulation vibrator if, for example, your g-spot placement, clitoral placement or the distance between your vaginal opening and clitoris varies from the anatomy the toy was designed for. Finding a dual stimulation vibrator that fits your anatomy may take lots of trial and error, and you may not find one. There's nothing wrong with you or your body if you can't seem to get a dual stimulation vibrator to work for you.

PENIS

Some vibrators are specifically designed for penis stimulation. These vary in shape and size – some are attachments to wands, some look like sleeves and require a person to penetrate them, and others cup around the penis. Some designs do require their user to have an erection when using them, so if you struggle to maintain erections due to HRT or have a post-phalloplasty penis without an erectile device, that's something to bear in mind when choosing a toy.

AIR PULSATION

Air pulsation toys aren't technically vibrators, but often also have vibration functions and are classed as vibrators by retailers, so I'm including them under the vibrator category. These clitoral toys are also sometimes called 'pressure wave' or 'suction' toys, although they don't actually produce any suction. Instead, they use pressure waves of air to create negative pressure and pulsations, which can feel like suction without actually touching the clitoris directly.

While these toys are intended for clitoral use, some people enjoy using them for nipple stimulation. The part of an air pulsation toy designed to fit around the clitoris can really vary in terms of size and shape, so people on testosterone especially should check measurements to make sure they can fit an air pulsation toy.

ANAL TOYS

Many toys that are intended for vaginal use can be used anally, but this is only safe if they have a flared base. If the base of the toy isn't wider than the largest part of the toy that will be placed inside a person, there's a risk of the toy becoming lost in the rectum.

Some toys are specifically designed for anal use. For the most part, these toys have flared bases by default, but because the sex toy industry is not regulated, some toys that aren't safe for anal use can still be sold as anal toys.

PLUGS

Anal/butt plugs are shaped like short dildos, with a flared base to prevent them from being lost up the anus. They vary in shape and size, with some plugs being curved for prostate stimulation, while others are a more simple, straight shape. Butt plugs come in a variety of sizes and can be weighted or vibrating, as well as made of glass or metal for temperature play. Some people use butt plugs to train for penetrative anal sex, others wear them during penetrative vaginal sex, and others simply like the sensation on its own.

BEADS

Anal beads are shaped like a set of balls on a string. In some cases, this is an actual string, which may be a hygiene issue even if the balls themselves are made of a body-safe material like silicone. Sometimes these beads are the same size, but at other times they may gradually increase in size. Unlike butt plugs, which are designed to stay in place, anal beads are meant to move in and out of the body to stimulate sphincter nerves.

STROKERS/MASTURBATORS

Strokers and masturbators are sex toys specifically designed to be penetrated. While most are made for people with average sized penises, there are a number of strokers created with testosterone bottom growth in mind, and even some designed for people with average sized clitorises. Strokers vary in level of realism, with some designed to look like body parts (like mouths of vulvas), others being more fantasy designs, and others being completely abstracted.

COCK RINGS

Cock rings are rings that are worn around the base of the penis and/or testicles. They can also be placed on dildos or other kinds of sex toys. The primary function of a cock ring is to aid in maintaining an erection. It does this by trapping blood in the penis, making erectile tissue harder for a longer period of time. They come in a huge variety of materials, from leather or neoprene to metal or silicone.

While cock rings are primarily intended to help in maintaining an erection, vibrating cock rings can be utilized in other ways. They can provide stimulation for a partner during penetrative sex, be worn on fingers to add stimulation to manual sex, or be placed on a dildo to turn it into a vibrating dildo.

STRAP-ON HARNESSES

Strap-on harnesses are harnesses designed to attach sex toys (primarily dildos) to a person's body. The most well-known kinds of strap-on harnesses attach dildos where a penis would be on the body, but others may attach a dildo to the thigh, hand or chin.

Strap-ons can be used by people of any gender, body and sexual orientation. Somebody may use a strap-on because they don't have a penis but want to penetrate a partner, or they have trouble maintaining an erection, or if using their penis for penetrative sex causes them to experience dysphoria, or for any number of other reasons. Harnesses can be fitted into four broad categories: underwear style, two strap, one strap, and harnesses for other parts of the body.

Underwear harnesses (as the name suggests) are designed to look like underwear, although they range in which style of underwear they look like. Underwear-style harnesses can feel easier to put on than other types, as there's no wrestling with straps, they are more easily washable between partners because they're made of fabric, and they tend to be less bulky than other styles. However, because their o-ring is sewn into the underwear and because fabric offers less support than straps, they're not well suited to large or heavy toys. Also, because they're not adjustable, they're not easily shared between partners with different bodies.

Two-strap harnesses have two straps that fit between the legs and resemble jockstraps. They tend to have multiple points of adjustment, making them more suited to sharing between people with different bodies. They offer more support for larger toys than underwear-style harnesses, and often have interchangeable o-rings. However, some people find the adjustment of straps difficult, or may dislike the bulk that two-strap harnesses can have.

If two-strap harnesses resemble a jockstrap, a one-strap harness looks like a thong, with one strap running between the wearer's legs. This single strap means the wearer may experience stimulation from their harness itself, and these types of harnesses are slightly less bulky than two-strap harnesses. However, it doesn't have as much security as a two-strap harness, so is less suited to larger toys or more vigorous play.

Harnesses exist for almost every part of the body you can imagine, from the chin (so that somebody can receive oral sex and penetration at the same time) to the thighs. Harnesses even exist for the hands, helping people who may have trouble gripping a toy.

PUMPS

Pumps are a kind of vacuum device, consisting of an acrylic cylinder or cup that fits over part of the body and a pumping mechanism. They aim to increase blood flow to the area, improving sensitivity. Pumps exist for many different parts of the body, including the penis, clitoris, vulva and nipples.

The results from pumping are immediate but temporary. Some transmasculine people claim that consistent pumping over long periods of time can increase bottom growth, although the evidence that this has any permanent impact is anecdotal.

Sex toys and you

Now we have an overview of what kinds of toys are available, how to choose a safe toy and some different ways that toys can be used, how do you figure out which sex toys are right for you?

First, all bodies are different and all sexual tastes are different. A toy that another person loves may not suit your tastes and preferences, and vice versa. It doesn't help that most sex toys are made with cisgender people's bodies in mind, so the ways in which we as trans people may want to use toys may not necessarily be reflected in discussions around them. The ways in which you want to use sex toys may not even be discussed here – it's impossible to address every issue people may have when using toys. Remember that you always have the option of adapting sex toys, rather than being limited by what and who toys are marketed for.

ACCESSIBILITY

Something important to consider when choosing a sex toy is your accessibility needs. Sex toy manufacturers often don't consider disabled people as potential consumers of their products in much the same way that they often don't consider trans people potential consumers of their products, and for those of us living at the intersection of these experiences, it can be doubly difficult to find the right toys for us.

What needs do you have when it comes to holding sex toys? Would a lighter sex toy that you still need to hold in place work for you, or do you need a hands-free toy? How large do you need buttons to be? If you're autistic, are there particular sensations that overstimulate you? If you have spasms and drop things as a result, would a toy that attaches to your hand or body work for you? What about a harness that attaches the toy to your body? If you have issues with reach, would a penetrative toy with a handle solve that issue?

QUESTIONS TO ASK WHEN CHOOSING A TOY

This isn't a complete list of all the questions a person could ask when deciding what sex toy to buy, but I hope they'll get you thinking about all the ways a toy could be right for you, as well as all the ways it might not be right for you.

Does your dysphoria inform the way you have sex and/or masturbate?
For many of us, dysphoria informs the way we have sex, both with partners and with ourselves. You may find that particular types of penetration, particular ways of being touched or being unclothed are dysphoria triggers for you. As a result, you might not want to use particular kinds of toys – like penetrative sleeves or cock rings – or may want to use a vibrator with your clothes on, meaning a more rumbly powerful vibrator is more suited to your needs. If you strap-on a dildo for sex, you might want a realistic toy that matches your skin tone, or you may want something totally non-representational. Everyone's dysphoria is different, and there's no wrong way for your dysphoria to impact (or not impact!) the ways you have sex.

Do you like penetration? What kind? What kinds of stimulation and sensation do you like from it?
If you like anal penetration, make sure that the toy you choose has a solid flared base. If you enjoy g-spot, a-spot or prostate stimulation (see *Chapter 2: Anatomy and Bodies*), a curved and firm toy might suit your needs. Some people like to play with temperature, and might prefer glass or metal toys. Weight can change the sensation of a toy – you might prefer a lighter silicone toy or a heavier metal one.

How girthy and long do you want your toy to be?
Remember, if you're planning on using your toy in a harness, get one that's a little longer, as some of the length is lost in the harness. Do you prefer a firmer toy – made of something like metal or silicone – or would you prefer cushier dual-density silicone?

What is your body's size and shape?
Sex toys are often designed with thin bodies in mind, and for those of us who are plus-sized and/or fat, this can cause challenges in use. Reaching over a larger belly may make it harder to use sex toys on genitals, for example. You may want to choose toys that have longer handles, or choose internal toys that are longer than you actually want to use for insertion, leaving some length usable as a handle. If you have thicker buttocks, you may want to choose toys with thicker and more sturdy bases when choosing an anal toy.

What's your living situation?
If you live with other people, this might mean you want a sex toy that's quieter or easier to hide. How much space do you have for storage? How much money do you have to invest in sex toys?

Has HRT impacted your genitals? How?
HRT (both oestrogen-based and testosterone-based) can have an impact on your genitals' shape, size and function. If you're on testosterone and have experienced bottom growth, you may find you no longer fit toys that are designed for cisgender women's clitorises, for example. If your HRT has made it more difficult to get or maintain an erection, you may want to choose toys that don't require the user to be erect. Alternatively, you may want to choose a toy that helps you maintain an erection once you've achieved one.

If you're post-surgery in any way, how has this impacted the way you experience sensation? Where do you feel sensation?
People with post-surgical bodies can experience differences in

what kinds of sensations they can feel, as well as what kinds of sensations are pleasurable. If you've had top surgery – either mastectomy or augmentation – you may experience some loss of sensation, particularly around incisions. While in most cases (for both procedures) people do regain some sensation, this may take time.

If you've had bottom surgery, different parts of your new genitals may regain sensation at different times. It's likely you won't regain sensation – or at least not to the level you had before – at the site of any surgical incisions. How might you be able to stimulate parts of your body where the sensation is new or different from what it has been before?

CHAPTER 5

Manual Sex and Grinding

In this chapter, I want to talk about manual sex – sex using hands, both penetrative and non-penetrative – and grinding, which I'll define broadly as external stimulation. While not everyone counts these as types of sex – and I think defining sex as 'something that feels like sex to me' is perfectly fine – I feel excluding it from this book would require a much more cisheteronormative definition of sex than one I would use, so I'm including it.

In this chapter, we'll talk about:

- ♥ tribbing, frotting and other kinds of grinding
- ♥ external manual sex
- ♥ muffing
- ♥ vaginal fingering (including post-op vaginas)
- ♥ anal fingering
- ♥ vaginal (again, including post-op vaginas) and anal fisting
- ♥ touching chests/breasts.

Tribbing, frotting and other kinds of grinding

First, what are tribbing and frotting? Both terms are used to refer to somebody grinding their genitals against a partner for sexual stimulation, although they have different implications around what body parts that person has, as well as where they are grinding. While 'frottage' generally refers to the act of rubbing any part of the body against the genitals of a partner, 'frot' or 'frotting' are predominantly used to refer to penis-to-penis contact. Similarly, 'tribbing' generally refers to vulva-to-vulva contact (sometimes called 'scissoring', although 'scissoring' is also used to refer to a specific position), but some people use it to refer to grinding the vulva on other parts of the body, like the thigh.

Tribbing and frottage aren't the only forms of sexual grinding – it's possible to grind against most body parts – and there's a lot of slang terms for this kind of sex, such as outercourse, dry humping or heavy petting. As with any sex act, some people can orgasm from grinding while others find it difficult or can't at all – if you find you can't orgasm from grinding, there's nothing wrong with you, and if you find you enjoy grinding despite being unable to orgasm from it, that's perfectly fine as well!

People enjoy grinding for many of the same reasons they enjoy any kind of sex – it feels good. For people who can't or don't want to have penetrative sex for any number of reasons (e.g. they experience dysphoria around penetration, have difficulty maintaining or gaining an erection, have vaginismus, or just find the experience uncomfortable or boring), grinding can still be on the table. If clothed, grinding also has a relatively low risk of STI transmission.

Friction is something to think about and play with during grinding sex. If fully clothed, it can be fun to try different fabrics – denim, for example, is a high-friction fabric that warms up with motion and provides a very different experience to a material like silk, which is low-friction. If grinding naked, adding lube reduces unwanted chaffing, especially if one or both partners are hairy.

Toys (see *Chapter 4: Toys and Gear*) can also be really fun to add to grinding. While there are a small handful of toys specifically designed for grinding, they aren't the only option at all. Wand vibrators pushed between bodies can stimulate both partners at once, double-ended dildos can allow two partners to experience penetration at the same time as grinding on each other, and some penetrable toys/sleeves are designed so that two people can penetrate them at the same time. As with all toys, so long as you're making sure any toy you use anally has a safe flared base, there are no rules about how toys can be used – if something feels good, it feels good.

While I mentioned that clothed grinding has a relatively low STI risk, this doesn't mean grinding has a zero STI risk. Some STIs transmit from skin-to-skin contact, and too much friction when grinding can cause micro-tears, increasing the risk of some STIs that are transmitted through fluid exchange. Vulva-to-vulva contact results in contact between partners' mucous membranes, and while *theoretically* this could be avoided by the use of a dam or other kind of barrier between bodies, this does limit movement, positions and what toys can be used. Getting tested and discussing your past, present and desired safer sex activities and boundaries with a partner is a more practical option.

External manual sex

'External manual sex' is a very technical way of saying 'using your hands on a partner's genitals without penetrating them'. There's a wide range of activities under this umbrella, from external anal massage to hand-jobs. However, as I said in *Chapter 2: Anatomy and Bodies*, a lot of types of tissue are analogous to one another, and medical transition often shifts people's bodies away from how society considers 'male' and 'female' bodies to how they look and function (if we were able to fit into these categories to begin with!). Because of this, I don't want to separate different 'types' of activity, and especially not by 'type of body'. However, something to bear in mind is that placing pressure on the scrotum can be more uncomfortable than placing pressure on the vulva, as hands can catch the epididymis (the tube that connects to the testicles) or knock testicles, if you have either or both of them. Depending on what implant was used, scrotal massage on a post-phalloplasty person can also both inflate and deflate penile implants.

Sex using hands (both externally and for the other kinds of sex I'll talk about in this chapter) can feel very intimate due to the level of sensation that hands have – each fingertip has more than 3000 touch receptors![21] Many of these receptors are primarily sensitive to pressure, which means it can be fun to play with for both active and receptive partners. If you're unsure how to touch a partner, it can be helpful to ask them to touch themselves and watch what they do. How many fingers do they use? Do they press down with the palm of their hand or the pads of their fingers? Do they angle to the left or right? Do they touch their erectile tissue (whatever form that may have) or do they prefer indirect stimulation? Do they enjoy their perineum being massaged? Are there ways of being touched that make them uncomfortable or dysphoric? Are any parts of their anatomy completely off limits for touch? Do they have scar tissue on their genitals that they do or don't want to be touched? What parts of their anatomy are more or less sensitive? (After bottom surgery, people may recover sensation in different parts of their genitals at different times.) These are all really valuable pieces of information about a partner – if you don't know the answers about yourself, it's worth taking some time to explore so that you can communicate them to your partner/future partners.

Depending on what you or your partner enjoy, some ways to involve hands externally include:

- Cupping the palm of your hand around a partner's genitals and massaging it with an even pressure – start with soft pressure and gradually increase it. Alternatively, you can maintain the same pressure, letting your partner grind against you for extra stimulation.
- Doing the same thing, but cupping around the perineum – the skin between the anus and genitals.
- Stroking down (or up!) their clitoris and/or penis shaft towards the glans. If your partner or you are more sensitive, playing with the hood or foreskin (if you have one) can make sensations less intense than touching the glans directly.

Muffing

Muffing is a term – first coined by Mira Bellwether in her 2010 zine *Fucking Trans Women* – that refers to penetrating the inguinal canals, which are channels behind the testicles that contain spermatic cords that connect the testes to the rest of the body. Muffing doesn't require being on hormones, and can be carried out both post-orchiectomy and post-vulvoplasty, with some people even saying they prefer it post-orchiectomy.

People with uteruses actually do have inguinal canals as well, although they contain a ligament that connects the uterus to the labia majora rather than spermatic cords, and are smaller. There is almost no information about whether the inguinal canals are accessible on those who have or have had uteruses, although I have heard anecdotal evidence for both yes and no answers.

It can be difficult to find the inguinal canals, as they're entirely covered by the skin of the scrotum and don't have any visible signs or markings – navigating by touch is easier than navigating by sight. Some people find they can find their canals more easily by pushing their testicles back inside their body. Muffing doesn't require lube, although it is a good idea to trim fingernails. There are a handful of reasons that some people enjoy muffing – it can feel affirming to be penetrated non-anally, some people enjoy the sense of fullness, and it can be used as a way to stimulate the ilioinguinal nerve. There a variety of ways to play with sensation when muffing, such as penetration with a finger, with a dildo or vibrator, pushing a testicle inside the body and letting it slide out repeatedly, or being penetrated in combination with oral sex. However, there are also plenty of people who don't enjoy the sensation or have mixed or negative feelings towards muffing, and it's perfectly fine to not be into it.

The inguinal canals can stretch over time, with some people able to take vibrators, dildos or penises. However, they generally start off relatively small, and forcing a stretch quickly can be quite painful and potentially weaken the walls of the inguinal canals.

Vaginal fingering

Vaginal fingering is possibly the most commonly known about form of manual sex – it was certainly the first I was ever aware of! I do want to highlight that I don't mention the a-spot in this section, as it's far more easily reachable with toys than it is with fingers – check out *Chapter 7: Vaginal Sex* to read more about that.

As with all kinds of sex, don't assume your partner is into penetration, and remember that just because somebody enjoys vaginal penetration at one point doesn't mean they'll always be into it. Lube is always a good addition to play, whether your vagina self-lubricates or not. Just as some people like penetration and some don't, different people like different kinds of things in their penetration – you or your partner may prefer gentle pressure or harsher pressured, curved fingers or straight fingers, gentle motion in-and-out or no motion at all. There's also the question of how many fingers somebody wants – everyone's body has a different capacity, so one partner may need easing up to four one finger at a time, while another may be able to only take two.

THE G-SPOT

The 'g-spot' isn't actually a single, distinct entity and, depending on individual anatomy, may be a single feature or a mix of features. What we do know is that it's located where the clitoris, urethra and vagina converge, around 5–8 cm from the entrance to the vagina, on the side closest to the belly. In some vaginoplasties, the prostate and other tissues are re-oriented so that they are located in a similar position. Part of the structure of the g-spot may come from the paraurethral sponge, a soft piece of tissue that surrounds the urethra, hence the name. It may also come from the internal clitoris.

The g-spot has a slightly different texture from the rest of the vagina – it's ridged and firmer, a lot like the roof of the mouth. G-spot stimulation can make some people feel like they need to pee, as it presses against the bladder. It can be pleasurable after this, although for some people g-spot stimulation remains uncomfortable. For those who enjoy g-spot stimulation, a classic move with the hands is the 'come hither' movement. Two (or three, in some cases) fingers are curled towards the receiver's belly, and the pads of the fingers stroked over it.

Anal fingering

As with vaginal fingering, anal fingering can serve as a warm-up for fisting, playing with toys and anal sex, or it can stand alone as its own act. If you are nervous about anal play – be it concern for hygiene, pain or something else – then it's worth checking out *Chapter 8: Anal Sex*.

Gloves and/or finger cots are highly recommended for anal

fingering. Not only do they make post-play clean-up easier, but they can also help to prevent the spread of STIs, and smooth the surface of the hands, for less friction and easier gliding. As with vaginal fingering, ask partners if they like penetration and how they prefer it. Lube is even more important for anal fingering than vaginal fingering, as the anus doesn't self-lubricate. The first few inches of the anus have the most nerve endings, so anal fingering doesn't need to be deep for the stimulation to feel good, although some people do specifically enjoy the sensation of their sphincters being stretched and the feeling of 'fullness' that large insertions can bring.

PROSTATE STIMULATION

The prostate is a small muscular gland, surrounded by sensitive nerve endings. Its main function is to produce seminal fluid, but it can also be massaged for sexual pleasure. As with the g-spot, some people find that a prostate massage makes them feel that they're about to pee. In some cases, people may lose erections during prostate massage, even if they enjoy the sensations, and not everyone ejaculates when they have a prostate orgasm.

The prostate can be stimulated externally through the perineum, although it may be difficult to actually feel the bulb. If massaged through penetration, the prostate is located about two inches from the entrance to the rectum, between the rectum and penis. Like the g-spot in the vagina, the prostate feels physically different from the rest of the rectal lining. The more aroused the person having their prostate massaged, the larger the prostate – which feels like a fleshy bulb – will be.

The same 'come hither' motion that works for g-spot stimulation also works well for prostate stimulation. However, it's worth noting that the prostate is further into the rectum than the g-spot is into the vagina, and in some cases people may struggle to reach it with their fingers, and find it much easier using toys.

A-SPOT STIMULATION
While anal fingering doesn't give direct access to the a-spot in the way vaginal fingering does, anal fingering can still put enough pressure on the a-spot to bring some people to orgasm. Other ways that people without prostates can orgasm from anal play include stimulation of the internal clitoris. Some people anecdotally say they enjoy anal penetration much more on testosterone HRT, which some folk wisdom theorizes is due to growth of the internal clitoris, but there is currently no scientific research that validates this claim.

There also currently isn't a huge amount of research about the anterior fornix erogenous zone, as it's technically known, but we do know that it's located further up the vagina than the cervix, in roughly the same place as the prostate. As with the g-spot, some people find that having it stimulated is uncomfortable, while others really enjoy the sensation. Because there isn't a huge amount of research on the a-spot even in cisgender women, we don't know a lot of trans-specific a-spot information, for example if it remains after a partial vaginectomy, or what the impact of cervix removal as a result of hysterectomy is on it.

Vaginal and anal fisting

Both vaginal and anal fisting often still carry a taboo, treated as a punchline rather than a sexual act that people mutually enjoy.

Sometimes called fist-fucking or handballing, it involves putting the whole hand into a vagina or anus. Fisting can be described, in many ways, as a more intense version of fingering, and a lot of the same advice can be given about fingering and fisting.

The person who is fisted – the fistee as I'll call them – and the person who does the fisting – the fister – can have as wide a variety of motivations and roles as in any other kind of sex. A fistee may enjoy a physical sense of fullness, may find that a fist places pressure on the g-spot, a-spot or prostate (see *Chapter 2: Anatomy and Bodies*), or may enjoy fisting because the communication it requires makes them feel safe and cared for. Similarly, a fister may enjoy making their partner feel 'full' for psychological reasons, may find it appealing as a service role, or may enjoy being able to physically feel their partner's responses and reactions in a way they can't with toys.

Fisting does come with some risks, as does any sex act, but these can be managed and risk of injury mitigated. For fistees, potential injury risks are long fingernails (which can be clipped or padded by wearing a nitrile/latex glove with cotton balls in the fingers), a lack of lubrication (which can be mitigated by using lube), or stretching/moving too fast (which can bruise or tear tissues). Tissue tearing also increases the risk of HIV or hepatitis C transmission – while fisting does have a relatively low risk of HIV transmission, it's still not zero. If a fister has open cuts on their hands (e.g. damaged nailbeds from nail biting), they can contract STIs if they come into contact with a fistee's mucous membranes or blood. Wearing gloves can mitigate this risk (see *Chapter 3: Sex and Safety*) with the added bonus that it reduces friction (especially if the fister has hairy hands) and prevents the fister's hands from absorbing as much lube.

When it comes to vaginal fisting, do bear in mind the impact that HRT and other hormonal changes can have on vaginal tissue, as well as the specifics of post-op vaginas. People on testosterone may find that their vaginal lining becomes thinner, they bleed more easily, and their vaginas find it more difficult to stretch to the size of a fist. Those who are post-hysterectomy may find they have a change in vaginal capacity and sensation, although some people do find they have more space in the vaginal capacity post-hysterectomy. People with post-vaginoplasty vaginas may also find some differences in their experiences – current surgical methods result in a vagina that is less elastic than non-op vaginas. While some post-vaginoplasty people find they *can* bottom for vaginal fisting, this is dependent on a lot of factors, and some people also find that they can't at all. Depending on who their surgeon is, people with post-op vaginas may be told to avoid anal fisting or anal sex for a period after bottom surgery to avoid vaginal prolapse and to avoid fistulas developing between the vaginal and anal linings.

Other factors that may impact whether somebody can be a fistee safely are experiencing pelvic inflammatory disease, recently having had a miscarriage or abortion, having muscular or skeletal injuries in the pelvic area, having healing genital piercings, having recently given birth, or being late in pregnancy. Menopausal and post-menopausal people may experience some of the same issues as people who go on testosterone in terms of vaginal atrophy, and they may require more lube and a slower approach. If in doubt, talk to a doctor.

In some cases, fisting can 'just happen', but the majority of the time it needs to be worked up to. Before a fist, try fingers and toys, slowly increasing in size, making sure to add more lube as necessary. While you may feel compelled to push yourself and rush to taking a fist, failing to take time to ease into the process risks damage and pain.

While the name 'fisting' leads some people to believe that fisting involves balling the hand up into a clenched fist, the shape a hand takes during fisting is flatter, and looks a little like a duck's beak. Once this 'beak' is slowly inserted, some people enjoy opening up their hand into a clenched fist shape, while others keep it in the original shape. While it's not advised when actually punching, tucking the thumb inside the fingers when a fist is clenched can avoid catching or tearing any tissue. Some fistees enjoy movement, like stroking or thrusting, especially against the g-spot, prostate or a-spot, but others may prefer no or minimal movement. Make sure to maintain clear and open communication with a partner, and if something doesn't feel right (emotionally or physically), you can always take things slowly, take a break or stop completely.

Some differences between anal and vaginal fisting – aside from the obvious – that are helpful to note are that the lining of the rectum is more delicate than that of the vagina, the anus lacks lubrication and it doesn't have an 'end' in the same way that a vagina does (be this a cervix or not). This means that lube is even more important than with vaginal fisting, and care needs to be taken stretching the anus. However, with time and care, a fister can use more of their arm anally fisting than vaginally fisting.

Touching chests/breasts

While I've focused on the anus and genitals in this chapter, hands can be used for sensual and sexual touch on all parts of the body. I'll talk about hands-in-mouth play in *Chapter 6: Oral Sex*, and erotic body massage is such a broad topic that it could (and has) filled an entire book on its own. Because of this, I'm going to focus on touch when it comes to chests and breasts specifically in this final section of the chapter, both because a lot of practicalities around touching chests also apply to other parts of the body, and because trans people often have complicated relationships to their chests. The chest is a part of the body that is heavily gendered – in some ways, because of its easier visibility to other people, it can feel more gendered than genitals. Whether it's informed by gender/trans status or not, everyone has a different relationship to their chest, and may only like their chest being touched in particular ways, may not like it being touched at all, or may love it being touched. As with all kinds of sex, communication is key.

Some things to bear in mind – as well as somebody's relationship to their chest/chest touch – include if somebody has recently started oestrogen HRT (meaning their nipples may be too sensitive for touch, or may be tender and feel sore more quickly/easily), and if somebody has scar tissue from surgery, be it mastectomy, breast implants, breast reduction or lumpectomy. Something else that can cause the formation of scar tissue is nipple piercing – while some people find that their nipples become more sensitive after piercing, others may lose sensitivity because of scar tissue. Additionally, nipple piercings take a long while to heal, and are vulnerable to infection during the healing stage.

CHAPTER 6

Oral Sex

This chapter is about oral sex – using the mouth, lips or tongue to stimulate a partner's genitals, anus or, in some cases, using strap-on dildos or other toys for this. We'll cover:

♥ myths and general considerations when it comes to oral sex
♥ oral sex on vulvas (including on post-op vulvas and vaginas, as well as vulvas of people on testosterone)
♥ oral sex on penises (including post-op penises, as well as penises of people on oestrogen)
♥ oral-anal sex
♥ oral sex on sex toys.

Myths and general considerations about oral sex

As with all kinds of sex, there are a lot of widespread cultural myths about oral sex. These include (but aren't limited to): that oral sex doesn't require the use of safer sex practices, that oral sex is 'dirty', that either nobody can orgasm from oral sex or that everyone can, or that you have to deep-throat a penis for oral sex to feel good.

As mentioned in *Chapter 3: Sex and Safety*, there is no such thing as truly 'safe' sex, and oral sex is no exception. While there is no risk of pregnancy from oral sex, and some STI transmission risks are lower with oral sex than with penetrative anal or vaginal sex, this doesn't mean there are absolutely no risks. STIs can transmit from partner to partner through oral sex, and infections can be caused by bacterial cross-contamination between the anus and vagina. STIs are more easily transmitted if you have mouth sores or your gums bleed (although they can also be contracted through the throat), so flossing and brushing gently before oral sex can help. However, it's generally inadvisable to brush or floss immediately before oral sex, in order to minimize risk of creating trauma to the gum tissue – ideally, you should leave about two hours between cleaning teeth and having oral sex.

Oral sex is also no dirtier than any other kinds of sex, all of which can be messy in their own ways. Hygiene practices can have an impact on partners' enjoyment of oral sex (although it's worth noting that people have different preferences), but there is ultimately no way to make genitals taste like anything except genitals. Over-washing can have negative impact on genital health, especially vaginal and vulva health. As with all kinds of sex, what makes somebody orgasm varies. Some people are able to orgasm from oral sex, while some people aren't, and some people are able to only under specific circumstances. And, finally, there are plenty of parts of penises that are sensitive and that don't require deep-throating to stimulate.

Oral sex on vulvas

While I've put them as separate headings, there is actually a lot in common between oral sex on vulvas and on penises. Both the clitoris and penis are phalluses, and with the variations in size and function that different bodies have (as well as the variation in how different trans people want to be touched) a randomly selected penis might have more in common with a randomly selected clitoris than another randomly selected penis. Some information may be repeated across both these sections, and you might benefit from reading both sections no matter the genitals you and your partners have.

VARIATION IN ANATOMY AND PREFERENCE
Some people find it easy to orgasm from oral sex, while others find it difficult. Orgasm doesn't have to be the goal of oral sex, but for some people it is a primary motivator. Different people enjoy different kinds of stimulation, different amounts in pressure, and have different areas that are more or less sensitive.

Post-vaginoplasty or vulvoplasty vulvas are very similar to non-op vulvas, with one exception – a post-op clitoris doesn't have as much internal structure as a non-op one. In practice, this means you might spend less time and attention on the clitoral shaft and more on the clitoral glans, and some of the tips for combining penetration with oral sex might not apply, but very little else.

Some types of touch can feel gendered, with this gendering resulting in dysphoria for some people. Some transmasculine people prefer receiving oral sex focused on suction around the clitoris/phallus, or prefer different language around oral sex.

That said, as with everything to do with sex, there's a lot of variation between people.

TECHNIQUES

As with other kinds of sex, warming up can make the experience of oral-vulva sex more enjoyable. In this context, that means paying attention to the whole vulva, rather than going directly towards the clitoris. Different people like and dislike different kinds of sensation when it comes to oral sex, so it's always helpful to ask, but some of the ways you can play with the whole vulva include tugging gently on the labia (in post-op vaginas, this stimulates what was once scrotal tissue, making it extra enjoyable), or using a flat tongue to lick around the clitoris or vaginal opening.

Even when stimulating the clitoris, it's not always necessary (or pleasurable) to go for the glans first. The clitoris is a phallus, and like phalluses of all sizes, it has a shaft. Stimulation along the shaft – be it through licking, pulling at the clitoral hood like a foreskin, or with the lips – can actually feel more pleasurable than direct glans stimulation for some people.

Variations in pressure, motion and speed of motion can all change how good an experience oral sex is, and as with everything, a lot of it is personal preference. Different people enjoy different levels of pressure, a flat tongue or a pointy tongue, direct glans stimulation or stimulation of the clitoral shaft, a focus on suction or a focus on tongue action. The general rule of thumb is variety – to find out what works for a specific person – and then consistency.

Some people swear by something called the Kivin method, which involves approaching the vulva horizontally, meaning that stimulation on the vulva is side-to-side rather than up-and-down. This does make it easier to stimulate more of the vulva than just the clitoris, which can make oral sex feel more pleasurable for some people, and help them reach orgasm faster. While it won't necessarily work for everyone, some people swear by it.

PENETRATION

We talked about penetration using hands in *Chapter 5: Manual Sex and Grinding* and will talk about using toys for vaginal penetration in *Chapter 7: Vaginal Sex* in a bit more detail, but I still want to discuss it a little here. I definitely sound like a broken record, but ask your partner before introducing penetration alongside oral sex – even people who love both vaginal penetration and receiving oral sex may not want the two to become combined, and some people may have a vulva but no vagina. If your partner has an internal clitoris, penetration can be used to stimulate the clitoral legs. For some people, this can result in squirting, where a substance is released (and 'gushes') from the Skene's glands.

POSITIONS

The major considerations when it comes to choosing a position for oral-vulva sex are the ability of the giver to breathe, the giver's neck comfort, pressure for the receiver, and the receiver's physical comfort.

Because oral-vulva sex involves close contact between two bodies – especially if the receiver prefers or needs significant pressure – breathing can sometimes become difficult, with both nose and mouth covered or otherwise occupied. Some physical positions make breath regulation easier for the giver, although breathing out of the sides of the mouth can make it easier in almost all positions.

Breathing can be an especially important consideration with 'receiver on top' positions, sometimes also called queening. It does reduce the pressure on the giver's neck, and provides people who like to grind plenty of opportunity to do so. However, things like pubic hair, a fleshier mons or a larger belly can take some manoeuvring, and it can be an emotionally intense position for some people. Dental dams also don't work well in this position, and if the receiver produces a lot of lubrication or is a squirter, this can add additional challenge. Also make sure that the giver has a way to communicate they need an out quickly – I and my partners tend to go with a double tap of the thigh.

'Missionary'-style positioning does alleviate some of these issues, although it can also be hard on the giver's neck. Giving oral-vulva sex from behind – with the receiver on all fours – can also be a challenge in its own right, as there's a longer reach to get to the clitoris, but can produce pressure that's enjoyable for both giver and receiver, even if it's not ideal for somebody who primarily wants suction.

OTHER TIPS

Some people enjoy oral sex while on their period, while other people dislike it, or can find it makes them dysphoric. Mess can be an issue with all kinds of period sex, so it's wise to put dark coloured towels down first. The fluid produced during a period is mostly blood, so oral sex with somebody on their period does have a chance transmitting STIs like HIV or hepatitis. PEP or holiday PrEP is something you may want to look into – check out *Chapter 3: Sex and Safety* for more information on this and other ways to mitigate some transmission risk. For people who are extra anxious about transmission risk or don't want to see their menstrual fluid because of dysphoria, wearing a tampon or menstral cup can be helpful, although take care with any penetration that takes place alongside oral sex.

Oral sex on penises

VARIATION IN ANATOMY AND PREFERENCE

Trans people may have trouble with or be unable to get an erection for a number of reasons: HRT making it difficult to gain or maintain an erection, a post-phalloplasty penis not having an erectile device implanted yet or at all, or just anxiety from dysphoria making it difficult. Despite the cultural image we have of oral-penis sex (often exclusively about hard penises penetrating somebody's mouth), oral sex is a lot more varied than this and an erection is absolutely not necessary for oral sex on a penis.

As outlined in *Chapter 2: Anatomy and Bodies*, there's a huge amount of variation in post-op penis anatomies. Some people with post-op penises keep their vaginal opening, some have a scrotum created, and some do only one or neither of these things. When it comes to post-phalloplasty penises, some people have their original phallus buried in the new one, some keep them separated, and people choose to have different erectile devices, or none at all. If somebody has a metoidioplasty or doesn't have their original phallus buried in their post-phalloplasty penis, most of what I talk about when it comes to general tips in this chapter will apply. However, there may be some differences, as post-metoidioplasty penises and non-buried clitorises are

smaller than the average penis and still have an internal structure, which can be stimulated alongside external anatomy. Some
people who do leave their clitoris unburied find that scrotal
stimulation can both stimulate their clitoris and feel affirming.
Pressure at the base of the post-phalloplasty penis can also put
pleasurable pressure on the non-buried clitoris.

If somebody has had their clitoris buried in their post-phalloplasty penis, they may find it easier to experience erotic sensation towards the base of the penis, not on the glans. However,
after healing, many people experience both tactile and erotic
sensation throughout their penis (it can be patchy, so ask your
partner where feels best), and a few people do find they actually
experience a lot of sensation at the head. Again, results and
sensation vary between people, as does what types of stimulation people actually enjoy. As with non-burial post-phalloplasty
penises, scrotal stimulation can help to specifically target the
buried clitoris, often through a tugging motion.

TECHNIQUE

As I mentioned at the beginning of the section on oral sex on
vulvas, there isn't a clear line between different kinds of genitals, and a lot of the techniques outlined in that section will
also work for people with penises if applied to analogous tissue
and structures, including the general tip of 'variety and then
consistency'. In non-op penises, the most sensitive part of the
penis tends to be the glans and the frenulum (the band of tissue
that connects the foreskin to the glans). However, just as plenty
of people don't like their partners going straight for the clitoral
glans, plenty of people don't enjoy their partners going straight
for the penis glans. Other ways to stimulate penises involve

licking or tugging on scrotal skin (if they've had a scrotoplasty and have a buried clitoris, this can be an excellent way to stimulate the buried clitoris) or along the shaft.

If you do want to have penetrative oral sex, you can use your tongue in combination with movement to create extra sensation, warmth and texture. Generally, keeping the tongue soft during motion, only switching to using it for more direct stimulation when you reach the most sensitive part of the penis (be this the glans and frenulum or near the base), helps to maximize sensation. You can also use a vibrator to take on the role of the tongue, placing it either under the frenulum (which can be easier if a penis is soft and more malleable) or towards the base of the penis and using your mouth to stimulate the rest of it.

If a penis is soft, it can be easier to move in a way that makes accessing particular sensitive spots easier. It can also make using a dental dam easier, as you can press a penis against the stomach. Depending on what erectile device somebody has chosen (if any), you may want to be careful about stimulation of a post-phalloplasty penis' scrotum because the area around testicular pumps can feel more sensitive, and can make rougher stimulation uncomfortable. The level of suction that people enjoy also varies, with penises that have a foreskin generally needing less stimulation and more easily finding suction uncomfortable.

USING YOUR HANDS

As with oral-vulva sex, oral-penis sex doesn't have to strictly involve the mouth, but can also involve use of hands. In some cases, this may be penetrative, with hands used for vaginal or anal penetration, as well as muffing. Hands can also be used to stimulate the penis (shaft or head), scrotum or perineum. If the person giving oral sex has their partner's penis in their mouth and is in motion, moving the hands in tandem can create a sense of simultaneous and seamless motion, as well as allow the giver to control the depth of penetration, and take time to breathe without disrupting the sensation/stimulation. You can also use your hands on the glans, pressing down with even pressure while focusing attention on the shaft, or gently tug at the scrotum (particularly in order to stimulate the original clitoris in a post-phalloplasty penis, buried or not).

POSITIONS

Different physical positions can make different kinds of stimulation easier, although as with oral-vulva sex, breathing can be an important consideration. There's a lot of variation, but a few common and broad position categories include receiver on their back or side, receiver standing while the giver kneels in front of them, and positions with the giver on their back.

Positions with the giver on their back work well for deep penetration, with the receiver able to thrust into their partner's mouth. Depending on the direction they face, they may also be able to simultaneously touch their partner's body, or even give them oral sex at the same time. A variation on this is teabagging, a position where the person receiving oral sex straddles the giver's face, receiving stimulation of the testicles. While this kind of sex often gets treated like a joke, it is a real and pleasurable way that some people have sex, and can work very well for post-op people who want to stimulate their clitoris (buried or not) through scrotal stimulation. Positions with the receiver standing up can work in synthesis with existing power dynamics, and some people find can make their orgasms from oral sex more intense, but do make it slightly more difficult to incorporate scrotal, vaginal, perineal or anal stimulation at the same time.

OTHER TIPS

If your partner ejaculates – not everyone with a penis does, and even if they do, it may differ from the average cis man's ejaculate in terms of taste, texture and consistency – decide whether you want them to ejaculate in your mouth or not. It is completely fine to not want somebody to ejaculate in your mouth, and it's good to tell your partner this ahead of time to set expectations clearly. When they approach orgasm, look for other ways to stimulate them to orgasm. Using your mouth on other parts of their genitals and using your hand to stimulate them more directly is one, as is using another part of your body to grind on or apply pressure to their genitals, or using a toy on them.

Deep penetration that reaches the throat (known as deep-throating) is not something that everyone enjoys, finds comfortable or wants to do, as it can trigger the gag reflex. Some people actually enjoy gagging specifically, but for people who don't and who still want to deep-throat, ways to make the process easier include experimenting with positioning and angles (positions with elevation generally work best), using lots of lube, remembering to breathe through the nose, and training the gag reflex over time to relax.

Oral-anal sex

There are a ton of slang terms for oral-anal sex (or analingus), including eating ass, tossing somebody's salad, and rimming.

Anal-oral sex can be entirely external or can also involve penetration, be it with the tongue, fingers or a toy. As we talked
about in *Chapter 5: Manual Sex and Grinding*, the anus has many
nerve endings (as does the perineum), which can make oral-anal
sex feel pleasurable. Some people also enjoy playing with the
cultural taboo around oral-anal sex, getting some excitement
from doing something that society deems 'naughty' or 'dirty'.
Some people are able to orgasm from rimming alone, although
plenty of other people require extra stimulation in order to be
able to orgasm.

HYGIENE

We'll talk about cleaning for anal sex in full depth in *Chapter 8:
Anal Sex*. However, I do want to also discuss it here, as oral-anal
sex does come with some risks. Small traces of faecal matter in
the anus and rectum – often too small to see – can transmit STIs
from partner to partner, or from anus to vagina if oral-vaginal
sex is carried out after oral-anal sex. One way to mitigate the
risks of oral-anal sex is to use a dental dam (see *Chapter 3: Sex
and Safety*). However, some people find that dental dams reduce
sensation, and they can be awkward to hold in place.

If you choose not to use a dental dam, you should wash
prior to oral-anal sex, even if just externally. Some people choose
to use an enema before oral-anal sex (see *Chapter 8: Anal Sex*
for more information), although this isn't always necessary. As
well as reducing the chances of coming across unexpected faecal
matter, cleaning out like this can sometimes reduce some of the
anxieties participants may have around anal play.

POSITIONS

Finding the right position for oral-anal sex makes everyone more comfortable, mitigating the neck cramps that a rimmer can experience, as well as the pain a rimmee can feel from awkward positions. Positioning pillows, as with all other kinds of sex, can help make positions more comfortable, elevating hips and providing support to a person's core.

From behind – similar to 'doggy style' – is the classic go-to position for oral-anal sex. Unlike positions like face-sitting, it avoids pressure on the rimmer's face, and allows for oral-anal sex to be combined with other kinds of stimulation and/or penetration. Angling or holding in position can sometimes be a challenge, which the rimmee lying flat on their stomach can sometimes mitigate. Another common position – which the positioning pillows mentioned earlier can really assist with – is with the rimmee on their back, legs spread and/or tucked upwards, and their butthole tipped upwards.

As with other kinds of oral sex, face-sitting – with the receiver squatting over the giver – can be fun to explore, although again balance can be an issue. Closing the distance between the rimmer's face and rimmee's anus with a pillow under the head can be helpful, as can the receiver using a bed or wall to maintain their balance.

TECHNIQUE

As with all kinds of sex, there's no 'one true way' to engage in oral-anal sex, and it's important to listen to feedback and respond to it. If you want to experiment with a partner, it's worth knowing there are many ways to explore anal sensation.

Beyond licking with the tongue, you can utilize your lips,

nose and chin. Even breath can feel sensual and sexy! Using other parts can also give your tongue a break if it starts to feel tired.

Flattening your tongue creates a larger surface area, meaning each movement has more pressure behind it. More pressure doesn't always mean better, so experiment with pressure alongside speed and direction. That said, it's worth making sure you allow your partner consistent time with each technique, rather than always moving from one to the next.

OTHER TIPS

While silicone lube can be excellent for other kinds of anal sex (so long as it doesn't involve silicone toys!), it not only tends to taste bad but remains as a glob, as it doesn't get broken down by spit or dry out. Water-based lubes are a better alternative and can, as always, reduce friction and make movement of the rimmer's tongue and lips and/or penetration of the rimee's butt smoother and easier. Some people like to use flavoured lubes during anal-oral sex, although it's worth checking if they contain glycerin (see *Chapter 4: Toys and Gear* for a discussion of lube ingredients to avoid).

Some people prefer removing the hair around their anus before oral-anal sex. As with any kind of body hair removal, it's entirely your choice. If somebody chooses not to remove their hair, this does make washing more important, as hair can trap things like small pieces of toilet paper.

Oral sex on toys

As well as oral sex on genitals or anally, some people enjoy performing or receiving oral sex from strapped-on dildos. Some people use the term 'faux job' to refer to this act, although I don't personally like the implication that strapped-on dicks are never 'real', so will use the term 'strap-on blowjob' in this section.

There are some toys that allow the wearer to get some sensation from strap-on blowjobs, with specialist dildos allowing for the transference of suction, and some grindable bases that can be attached to toys, allowing the wearer to feel pressure on their toy. Some stand-to-pee devices can also be used in this way – if they're cupped around a vulva, the wearer can feel some suction around the tip. Even without additions, strap-on blowjobs can involve pressure on the mons and/or clitoris or penis, which can be pleasurable and, in some cases, lead to orgasm.

Outside direct stimulation, some people enjoy strap-on blowjobs because it helps them focus on other sensations involved in sex. Some people enjoy receiving strap-on blowjobs in combination with other kinds of stimulation – like anal or vaginal penetration, muffing or using a vibrator – but others may dislike or even hate it. For some, strap-on blowjobs may be connected to power exchange and power play (see *Chapter 9: Kink*) or gender, while for others they may have absolutely nothing to do with each other. Some people swear by strap-on oral sex as a good way to get used to wearing a strap-on, as it offers a lot of versatility in positioning and is less taxing compared to anal or vaginal strap-on play. The act is as varied as the people who do it.

Strap-on oral sex is very safe as far as sex acts go. The only

STI risks are related to sharing toys and using toys made of unsafe materials (see *Chapter 4: Toys and Gear*). There is a risk of throat irritation, as materials like silicone can be a bit more rough on the throat tissue than flesh-and-blood penises. This can be mitigated to an extent by choosing softer density or dual density silicone toys, and/or by drinking a throat-soothing beverage afterwards.

The right harness for strap-on blowjobs is the one that feels right to you. A too-large harness can result in a dildo that shifts too much in use, while a too-small harness can be uncomfortable. Jock-style or two-strap harnesses usually leave genitals accessible for play, while underwear-style harnesses can make oral sex feel more 'natural'. You can even not use a harness at all, and simply hold a dildo against your body. While the same 'choose what you prefer' point does apply to dildos, softer dildos or dual density toys (which have a soft and pliable outer layer) can feel more comfortable for the person giving oral sex. Silicone is sanitizable in a way that other materials like TPE aren't, so using toys made of silicone and cleaning between partners/uses can mitigate STI transmission risk. Because oral sex on a dildo can be a bit rougher, lube can be really helpful, especially for people who experience dry-mouth. Flavoured lubes can be a fun addition to strap-on blowjobs, although many contain glycerin, so tread carefully if you're planning on using the same toy for vaginal sex after, as introducing glycerin to the vagina can contribute to yeast infections.

CHAPTER 7

Vaginal Sex

In this chapter, we'll talk about vaginal sex. Unless otherwise specified, the advice in this chapter applies to both non-op and post-op vaginas, as well as the non-op vaginas of people both on and not on HRT.

We'll cover:

- positioning for vaginal sex
- general penetrative vaginal sex
- penetrative vaginal sex with toys or prosthetics
- PiV (penis-in-vagina) with non-erect penises
- PiV sex with bottom growth and/or post-metoidioplasty penises
- mutual vaginal penetration
- vaginismus.

Positioning

Missionary – with the receptive partner on their back and the penetrative partner between their legs – is a classic for many reasons, one of the key ones being it allows for face-to-face and body contact. With some adaption, missionary works well for thigh harnesses as well as more 'conventional' strap-on harnesses, and this isn't the only way missionary can be adapted. Placing pillows (specific positioning pillows or general) under the receptive partner's hips allows for deeper penetration and can work well for penetrative partners whose penises angle downwards, and if the penetrative partner rests on their knees, making space for an external vibrator can be much easier.

If the receptive partner has limits to how deep they want penetration or prefers penetration at very specific angles (which is perfectly normal – many non-op and post-op vaginas have a 'tilt' to them), positions with them on top can allow them to control exactly what kind of penetration they experience. This can also work well if the partner penetrating has difficulty moving their hips or thrusting for long periods of time, and can be adapted to both sitting and lying positions, as well as with partners facing each other or facing away.

Penetration from behind – with the receptive partner on their knees – works well for deeper penetration and can make direct g-spot stimulation easier. If this position is difficult to maintain over time, a positioning pillow or wedge can work wonders, although you can always adapt this by lying on your belly. Penetration from behind also allows the receptive partner to use a vibrator on themselves or directly touch their clitoris more easily, and allows for the penetrative partner to thrust with more intensity if they want.

Standing positions depend somewhat on body type – with partners of equal heights generally having an easier time, although height differences can be equalized by standing partners on furniture or a staircase – but can bring with them a very sexy sense of urgency. There's a lot of variations on standing positions, with factors like the amount of space you have, how much strength partners have, and partners' levels of flexibility. In general, standing positions do require leveraging of body weight for better stability, which could mean leaning against walls or resting against tables.

On the other end of the spectrum, spooning can require very little physical exertion. In the classic spoon, both partners lie on their sides, facing the same way, the receptive partner brings their knees up slightly, and the penetrative partner penetrates them from behind. This position can provide a feeling of closeness and intimacy, can work well for people who struggle with holding their partner's body weight, and makes accessing the clitoris for extra stimulation very easy.

Penetrative vaginal sex

Penetrative sex isn't the be-all-and-end-all to sex, even if our culture sometimes treats it that way, especially when it comes to penis-in-vagina sex. While there aren't currently any studies on the percentage of trans people who can orgasm from just vaginal penetration, we do know that up to 81.6 per cent of cis women can't orgasm from vaginal penetration alone.[22] However, just because something doesn't necessarily lead to orgasm doesn't mean that it's not pleasurable or desirable, and stimulation of the receptive partner's clitoris/penis (depending on your anatomy) during vaginal penetration is always an option. Some people do find that they can stimulate their internal clitoris through penetrative sex, and others may find they can have g-spot or a-spot orgasms (see *Chapter 2: Anatomy and Bodies* for a refresher if you need it), but this is a minority of people, so if you can't orgasm from vaginal penetration, there is absolutely nothing wrong with you.

Penetration with toys/prosthetics

Penetrative vaginal sex using a strap-on or prosthetic is generally quite similar to penetrative sex with an erect penis, with a few small exceptions. Because the toy or prosthetic isn't attached to the body in the same way, the wearer won't necessarily get the same kind of feedback, even if they're using a toy with some way to give the wearer feedback, like a base that grinds against them or a sleeve in the base. That's not to say there isn't some feedback – some people can feel their partner squeezing Kegel muscles around a toy/prosthetic – but because there isn't the same level of haptic feedback, open communication is even more important than normal.

If you're somebody who isn't used to topping, using a toy or prosthetic for the first time can engage some muscles you've rarely or never used before, and can be super tiring as a result! Newbies to topping may also thrust with their hips, which can be super tiring over time and feel too intense for some bottoms. Instead, try keeping the hips more still and thrust lightly. A strapped-on toy or prosthetic may also be a little more difficult to control than a permanently attached penis, so don't feel afraid to use hands to adjust or hold your cock in the right position.

Prosthetics and toys can also dig into the wearer's body – depending on the toy base and harness – and can even result in bruising after vigorous thrusting. If this happens, choosing a dildo with more cushioning or adding a cushioning base to a dildo may help (if you're in a pinch, a cup or egg-shaped masturbation sleeve can also work!), as may changing the harness to one that is less tight or is made of a material with less give, so it needs to be tightened less.

Penetration with non-erect penises

Penetrative sex is absolutely not the be-all-and-end-all of sex, but it can be something that people enjoy even if they are unable to or find it difficult to get or maintain an erection. Penetrative sex with a flaccid penis is completely possible, and is sometimes called 'stuffing'. It's easier with vaginal penetration than with anal penetration and, if somebody does have the capacity for erections, can sometimes lead to one. One issue with stuffing is that putting a condom on a flaccid penis can be difficult, although it is possible.

Other options for people who find it very difficult to get an erection, or can't because, for example, they may not have had an erectile device implanted into their post-phalloplasty penis (yet or at all), include hollow strap-ons, penis sleeves and sheaths and penis support devices. There are some slight differences between different options (strap-ons require the use of a harness or may have a harness built into them, a sheath covers an entire penis whereas a sleeve only covers the shaft, and support devices have minimal coverage), but they all serve the same purpose. You may prefer one option over another for reasons related to dysphoria, sensation, if you want to wear a condom, or aesthetics.

Penetration with bottom growth and/ or post-metoidioplasty penises

The clitoral growth that testosterone HRT often results in (see *Chapter 2: Anatomy and Bodies* if you need a refresher) can sometimes be used for penetrative sex. This is very dependent on a number of factors, including (but not limited to) bottom growth size, where bottom growth sits when erect, the body shape and size of both partners, how much tissue surrounds the top's bottom growth, how much tissue surrounds the receptive partner's entrance, and positioning. Penetrative sex with bottom growth is generally easier vaginally than anally, although penetrative anal sex with bottom growth is possible, and vaginal penetration may not be possible with some combinations of bodies.

Using a clitoral pump can make penetration easier, as increasing blood flow can make an erection firmer (and in some cases, make bottom growth temporarily a bit larger). If a clitoral release hasn't been performed and the ligaments are still in place, positions that result in bottom growth pointing down work well – think missionary with the receptive partner's butt raised by a pillow and their legs pushed back, although the receptive partner being on top ('cowgirl') also works well. Once penetration has been achieved, a grinding motion rather than thrusting motion works well to prevent the bottom growth from slipping out.

Post-metoidioplasty penises use already existing bottom growth, and have a lot of similarities in terms of safe sex and positioning. As with bottom growth, being able to have penetrative sex does depend on a number of factors, although some specialist penis extenders do exist for post-meta penises. If the phallus changes position during meta (be it from just a clitoral release or a mons resection), penetration can become possible from a wider range of positions.

Conventional condoms that fit either bottom growth or post-metoidioplasty penises can be difficult to find, and condoms alone may not completely mitigate the chance of STI transmission through vaginal sex if both partners still have a vagina. Depending on the penetrating partner's size, finger cots can be an alternative to condoms, although having the receptive partner wear an internal condom is also an option.

Mutual penetration

Two partners with vulvas (or one with and one without, although we'll talk more about this in *Chapter 8: Anal Sex*) can use double-ended dildos to engage in mutual penetration. We discussed safe sex toys and what you should look for in terms of materials in *Chapter 4: Toys and Gear*, although I would personally recommend looking specifically at silicone when it comes to double-ended toys, as they have more flex than other body safe materials, but can still be firm and unlikely to bend. Some double-ended dildos are sold as 'strapless strap-ons', but can be very difficult to keep in without a harness unless the person wearing it has very strong pelvic floor muscles.

There are some limitations when it comes to double-ended dildos. For example, standing positions can be more awkward than when using strapped-on toys or a penis. Depending on how close people plan their bodies to be, longer toys can reduce the chance of STI transmission. Alternatively, mutual penetration can be a fun addition to vulva-to-vulva grinding (see *Chapter 5: Manual Sex and Grinding*).

Vaginismus

Vaginismus is a condition where the muscles of a vagina tighten – outside the control of the person who has the vagina – during attempted penetration, making it painful and sometimes impossible. People can develop vaginismus even if they've previously enjoyed penetrative sex and found it pleasurable, or it may stem from a number of causes, including other medical conditions (such as thrush), anxiety disorders, medical trauma or unhealed prior surgery or other kinds of trauma. Some people find that they only experience discomfort with penetration in specific circumstances, while others experience it with any kind of penetration. The management or treatment of vaginismus depends heavily on the specific circumstances of each person – those with underlying trauma may benefit from therapy, while other patients may only need physical therapy that teaches them to relax their pelvic floor muscles. Some people use dilators to become more comfortable with vaginal penetration. And, of course, some people choose to just not have penetrative vaginal sex because it doesn't make a huge difference to their personal sex lives.

While historically there has been a perception that only cis women experience vaginismus, trans people of all kinds can experience this, including people with post-op vaginas. In fact, the physical trauma of surgery can sometimes become associated with penetration due to the post-op dilation process.

If vaginismus develops during the immediate post-operative period, it may resolve as healing continues, but if it continues after the healing period, it can be worth seeking out treatment in the form of therapy, learning relaxation techniques, and doing pelvic floor muscle exercises.

There's very little research on vaginismus when it comes to trans people specifically, but anecdotally I know people who have said that testosterone HRT made their vaginismus both better and worse. The vaginal atrophy that is associated with testosterone HRT can make penetration more painful, but can be mitigated with topical vaginal oestrogen creams.

CHAPTER 8

Anal Sex

I n this chapter, we'll talk about anal sex.
We'll cover:

- ♥ myths about and around anal sex
- ♥ preparing for anal sex
- ♥ positioning for anal sex
- ♥ prostate stimulation
- ♥ penetrative anal sex with toys or prosthetics
- ♥ anal sex with bottom growth and/or post-metoidioplasty penises.

Myths about anal sex

Anal sex has a lot of cultural misinformation around it due to a lot of factors, including homophobia and the fact that it's a kind of sex not focused on reproduction. Some of the myths around anal sex include (but aren't limited to):

- · It's normal for anal sex to hurt.
- · Anal sex is always dirty.

- Somebody without a prostate can't enjoy or orgasm from anal sex.
- Somebody who is on top for anal sex using a prosthetic or strap-on can't get pleasure from it.

Pain during anal sex is – as with all kinds of sex – a sign that something is wrong, and pleasurable anal sex should not hurt. If anal sex does hurt, this is potentially a sign that the receptive partner isn't relaxed or warmed-up enough, or that not enough lube is involved. Using a desensitizing lubricant may seem like a quick and easy way to avoid pain, but in reality means that your body isn't giving you any warning about potential harm or injury, possibly leading to worse harm or discomfort later on.

While there is always some chance of coming into contact with faecal matter during anal sex, the anus and rectum actually have very little faecal matter in them, as stools are held by the body in the sigmoid colon. Most penetration, unless notably deep, will not reach into the colon. The receptive partner emptying their bowels and washing their anus before sex, and the penetrative partner wearing a condom or gloves, is advisable, although the receptive partner can also use an enema (discussed in the 'Preparing for anal sex' section) if they wish.

While there is a persistent cultural myth that anal sex is only pleasurable to people who have prostates or whose prostates are most easily stimulated through anal sex, this isn't the case at all. The anus contains many nerve endings, such as the pudendal nerve, which extends throughout the pelvic area. Some people also find they can get a-spot stimulation from anal penetration. While pleasure isn't defined by orgasm, some people can orgasm from any of these kinds of stimulation, whether they have a prostate or not.

Finally, while pleasure during sex isn't limited to pleasure from physical sensation and stimulation, many people find topping with prosthetics or strap-ons sexy and pleasurable in its own right. However, there's also a possibility to get some kind of sensory feedback from topping, including adding things like a base to grind on or a bullet vibrator pocket in the harness.

Preparing for anal sex

If anal sex is new to you, it can be worth taking some time to prepare for it on your own before engaging in it with a partner. Aside from seeking out education about anal sex to dispel some of the myths and misinformation around it (congrats on picking up this book!) and talking with your partner about anal sex, it can be valuable to explore anal sex by yourself and at your own pace to begin with. Try exploring with just fingering to begin with, before trying small toys, making sure to use lube as the anus doesn't self-lubricate.

One of the fears people tend to have around anal sex is about the potential mess or potential contact with faeces. Ultimately, there is no way to completely guarantee that there won't be any contact with faecal matter, so the best thing to do is be prepared to deal with mess if or when it happens without shaming anyone involved. Some ways to reduce the likelihood of mess include eating a high fibre diet, emptying your bowels before play, and using soap and water or a wipe to clean externally.

Some people choose to douche (i.e. give themselves an

enema) before anal sex, especially if they're going to engage in deep anal penetration. While it's not necessary (and some douching methods can be harmful to the rectum or colon – more on that in a moment), it can help some people become more comfortable and give them peace of mind.

Using a bulb douche – which consists of a soft, squeezable bulb used to both hold water and propel it into the body and a nozzle – is the simplest method of douching. Pre-prepared enema kits often contain ingredients that can irritate or dry out the rectum, as they're often designed to treat constipation. Many people use warm tap water, which is fine for occasional use, but can damage the anal canal's lining and flush out necessary bacteria if used too frequently (the benchline is generally two to three times a week).

Douching generally should take place about an hour before anal sex, as if done too soon before anal sex, there is a chance that liquid that's been stuck in the folds of the anal canal can be released during sex. After lubing up and inserting the nozzle of a bulb douche (ideally squatting over the toilet or with one foot resting up on it), squeeze the bulb gently to push water into the rectum. Pushing fluid upwards rather than downwards means gravity is on your side in preventing too much liquid from entering the rectum. Once the liquid enters your anus, you will feel as if you have to poop, but hold it in for between ten and thirty seconds (by squeezing the pelvic floor muscles). After this, release the dirty water into the toilet.

Some people like to douche a second time or until water runs clear, but ideally you shouldn't douche too many times or use too much liquid. Douching too much in one session can cause water to end up in the colon, which is far more sensitive to damage and temperature. Water reaching the colon rather than just cleaning out the rectum is what's responsible for the phenomenon of water coming out clear and then coming out dirty on a subsequent wash. Shower douches – which attach to existing showers like a standard shower head – also have this issue, as they tend to be long and reach the colon. Additionally, because they don't have controllable pressure in the same way that a manual bulb douche does, they risk damage to the colon's tissues and microbiome.

Positions for anal sex

Many positions that work for vaginal sex also work for anal sex with a little adjustment, and vice versa. What positions you choose can depend on comfort with penetration, how deep you want penetration to be, if the receptive partner wants to experience prostate stimulation, how flexible both partners are and how able each partner is to support their weight and/or that of their partner.

Positions with the receptive partner physically on top allow them to control the depth and speed of any penetration or movement, with the option to face towards the penetrative partner's face or away. These positions also allow additional play to be incorporated easily, whether this is using a vibrator on the receptive partner's penis or clitoris, or the penetrative partner using their fingers for vaginal penetration. As with vaginal sex, positions with the receptive partner on top also give them control over the angle of penetration – making prostate stimulation easier – and can make sex easier for a penetrative partner who has difficulty moving their hips or thrusting for long periods of time.

Some positions that work well for shallow penetration – remember that most of the nerve endings of the anus are in the first two inches, so shallow penetration will still result in anal stimulation – include the receptive partner lying flat on their stomach, with the penetrative partner entering them from behind. Because this position doesn't require the receptive partner to hold their body up, it can also be a lot easier on their muscles. However, it can be more difficult to incorporate other kinds of play into this position – lying on top of a vibrator is possible, but if the receptive partner needs pinpoint stimulation or wants to use another kind of toy like a sleeve, it may be difficult. Another position that works well for shallow penetration but allows the receptive partner more freedom in other play involves them lying on their side, with the penetrative partner again penetrating them from behind, either kneeling or standing, if the receptive partner is on the edge of a bed or other elevated surface.

On the opposite end of the spectrum, positions that allow for deep penetration include a variation on the receptive partner lying on their stomach, where they instead bend their knees and slightly raise their hips. A pillow (specifically for positioning or otherwise) can make holding this position a lot easier. Another position that allows for deep anal penetration involves the receptive partner lying on their back, bending their legs and throwing them apart wider than shoulder length – gripping their feet can help with holding this. While the receptive partner's hands are likely to be occupied, this position does leave the penetrative partner with a free hand for other kinds of stimulation, and allows partners to see each other's faces.

Prostate stimulation

We talked about the prostate in *Chapter 2: Anatomy and Bodies*, but as a quick refresher it's a small gland (about the size and shape of a walnut) that some people have wrapped around the urethral canal, between the bladder and penis and towards the belly rather than the rectum. Its main function is producing a fluid that makes about 15 per cent of ejaculate, but the number of nerve endings it has mean it can also be very pleasurable to stimulate. For some people with post-vaginoplasty vaginas, the prostate may be most easily stimulated through the vagina, which is sometimes positioned so that the prostate can serve as a g-spot. However, the most common ways to stimulate the prostate are from external stimulation of the perineum or through anal penetration.

The exact location of the prostate varies by person, but in most cases it can be located around 2–3 inches inside the rectum, towards the stomach. This can make it difficult to reach with fingers, although if you or a partner can reach it with fingers, a curved 'come hither' pose and movement works best. If you can't reach the prostate with your fingers, toys like prostate massagers, curved or weighted anal plugs (although other styles of plug can also stimulate the prostate) or curved dildos are all alternative options. Toys designed for g-spot stimulation can generally be utilized for prostate stimulation (*if* they have a flared base), but you may find that the shape of some isn't quite curved right to reach the prostate.

As with every kind of sex, learning how to have prostate orgasms can be a process, and it's helpful to take time to explore it by yourself before engaging in prostate play with a partner. When stimulating the prostate manually, try experimenting with movements, like up and down strokes, side to side movements, or drawing circles with your fingers. Dildos can be gently rocked for prostate stimulation, or can be used to thrust. When thrusting for prostate stimulation (with a dildo, prosthetic or penis), you will likely need to specifically angle it at the prostate – because the prostate is accessible via the *wall* of the rectum, thrusting directly into the rectum can miss it entirely. Something else to consider when it comes to choosing a dildo for prostate stimulation is the balance between firmness and softness – a too-soft toy may not be able to provide enough steady pressure to the prostate, but a too-hard toy may feel uncomfortable. While curves are useful for toys that are more gently rocked against the prostate, a large curve may make the movement of thrusting awkward.

Anal sex with toys or prosthetics

Anal sex using a strap-on or prosthetic isn't too dissimilar from anal sex with a standard issue penis or from vaginal sex using one. However, there are a few minor differences worth consideration. The lining of the anus is more delicate than the lining of the vagina, and so is easier to damage. The lack of physical feedback that a prosthetic or toy gives means that a little more caution and preparation can be needed when having anal sex using them.

A second difference is the strength of the anal sphincters compared to that of the Kegel muscles. This is most relevant when it comes to double-dildos, including so-called 'strapless strap-ons'. These toys use the strength of the wearer's pelvic floor muscles to keep them in place, which can be a challenge at the best of times, especially if they produce a lot of lubrication, and it becomes even more difficult when any kind of movement or motion gets added. Because the anal sphincter is much stronger than even-toned Kegel muscles, there's an added level of challenge in keeping the toy in place. Using a strapless stap-on in a harness can help keep the toy in place and add some stability.

Anal sex with bottom growth or post-metoidioplasty penises

Penetrative anal sex with bottom growth is not impossible, and is significantly more difficult than penetrative vaginal sex using the same anatomy. Doing so is also a lot more dependent on anatomical and positioning specifics, as there is a larger distance to reach the anus between the buttocks than there is to penetrate a vagina when pressed against the vulva. Generally, penetrative anal sex with bottom growth or post-metoidioplasty penises is a lot easier if the bottom has spent some time stretching their anus, as a small gape can make penetration far easier.

Safer sex is very important with anal sex involving bottom growth or post-metoidioplasty penises, especially if the person involved has not had a vaginectomy or their urethra lengthened.

While people with all kinds of penises can contract a UTI from topping during unprotected anal sex, a shorter urethra makes UTI infections more likely, and the introduction of bacteria from the anus into the vagina can also cause vaginal infections. The safest option for those who want to top for anal sex with bottom growth or a post-metoidioplasty penis is to have the receptive partner use an internal condom. While these devices were and sometimes still are called 'female condoms', implying they are for vaginal use only, they can also be used for anal sex.

As with the 'strapless strap-ons' discussed earlier, penis extensions made for post-metoidioplasty penises or for bottom growth may be less suitable for anal sex than they are for vaginal sex. While they don't rely on the strength of pelvic floor muscles to stay in place, the force they need to stay in place is still up against the strength of the anal sphincter.

CHAPTER 9

Kink

I n this chapter, we'll talk about:

- ♥ what kink is
- ♥ some of the ethical and conduct frameworks associated with kink
- ♥ the importance of consent and communication during kink play
- ♥ some of the ways in which people enjoy playing with kink.

This chapter isn't a complete guide to kink, because there's so much under the kink umbrella that it can't be covered in a single chapter – it would take many books to discuss everything to do with kink, and even then something would definitely be missed! However, I will try to give a broad overview of terminology and theory, as well as discuss some practical notes on a handful of kink practices.

What is kink?

In the broadest terms possible, 'kink' refers to any sexual practice or desire outside the norm. If you're thinking this sounds incredibly non-specific and contextual, it is! What's considered 'kinky' varies wildly across time, place and different communities. In some communities, acts like anal sex or strap-on play would be considered kinky, despite the fact that on a personal level I don't think they are (and, in honesty, think considering them 'kinky' is rooted in cisheterocentrism).

However, I do have to define kink in order to write this chapter. With the disclaimer that I cannot account for every individual's line of what is considered 'normal' sexuality, I'm going to be working with the definition of kinky as a kind of sexual play (although it does not necessarily need to involve or be thought of as 'sex') or erotic expression that plays with power, sensation, role or fantasy, as well as scenarios that involve more than one of these aspects.

Kink vs BDSM

Some people use the terms 'BDSM' and 'kink' interchangeably. BDSM in this context is an acronym that stands for: bondage and discipline, domination and submission, and sadism and masochism.

While I think BDSM is a sub-category of kink, I don't think the two are interchangeable. For one, not all kink or fetish involves any of these aspects – somebody might, for example, have a kink or fetish for a particular material or body part completely without any BDSM aspects. Second, BDSM is a relatively recent term, only coming to prominence as a community umbrella term in the 2000s, and is still not always the preferred terminology for all communities that gather around kinky sex. A lot of communities still use 'SM' (the most common umbrella term from the 1970s until BDSM took over in the 2000s) or 'leathersex'. I also think using the term BDSM can imply that these interests come as a package deal, when the term originates more as a 'coalition' of different kink interests and groups. An interest in sadism and masochism, for example, doesn't necessitate an interest in bondage, or in playing with power in a dominant/ submissive scenario.

Language and definitions

So these terms – bondage, discipline, dominance, submission, sadism, masochism, top, bottom and so on – what do they specifically mean?

BONDAGE
'Bondage' is an umbrella term for different techniques that involve tying up or restraining a partner. There's a huge variety of methods and tools that can be used for bondage, from rope or cuffs to pieces of clothing. While some people enjoy bondage as part of playing with power, others may enjoy it purely for sensation reasons.

DISCIPLINE
In the context of kink, 'discipline' refers to the practice of setting

rules, primarily in a dominant/submissive dynamic. Some people argue that the prominence of discipline comes from the gay
biker clubs that formed the origin of the leather community,
with men drawing on their military experiences during the
Second World War.

DOMINATION AND SUBMISSION

Domination and submission are complementary roles in some
kinds of BDSM, where one party expresses power over another.
This may be through the creation and enforcement of sets of
rules, carrying out rituals or any number of practices. For some
people, dominant/submissive (sometimes stylized as Dominant/
submissive or D/s) are set roles within their relationship, whereas
for others they may last only as long as a session (or 'scene') does.

SADISM AND MASOCHISM

Sadism and masochism (sometimes stylized as SM, S/M or
S&M) refers to sexual practices involving or sexual enjoyment of
inflicting and receiving pain. Not all masochists enjoy all kinds
of pain – somebody might, for example, enjoy being flogged but
hate receiving wax play. While dominants are often assumed to
be sadists and submissives masochists, this isn't always the case.
The D/s dynamic may contain little or no SM play, some SM play
may involve no D/s dynamic, or the dominant in a D/s dynamic
may be a masochist.

DOM/SUB VS TOP/BOTTOM

Domination and submission refer to complementary aspects of
power play. While some people use the terms 'dominant' and
'submissive' to refer to 'the partner who initiates play' and 'the

partner who is responsive in sex' respectively, this isn't always the case. A dominant may be a bottom and a submissive partner a top. The simplest explanation that I use is that dom/sub is about power, while top/bottom are about action – a dominant 'leads' while a top 'does', a submissive 'follows' while a bottom 'has things done to them'.

Risk, consent and communication

Kink is, in many ways, a riskier kind of sex. Much of what I said in *Chapter 3: Sex and Safety* also applies to kinky sex, but there's also an added layer of risk emotionally, mentally and physically.

There are lots of approaches to managing the specific risks of kink play. In this section, we'll discuss what some of the risks of BDSM and kink are, how to negotiate consent within kink and how to communicate risks, desires and our emotions about kink, both before and during play.

SSC AND RACK

BDSM and leather communities have been creating ethical and conduct acronyms as a way to navigate the risks of kink for a very long time. Some of the more common acronyms currently in use (at least in predominantly English-speaking kink/leather communities) are 'SSC' and 'RACK'.

SSC is the older of the two acronyms, created in 1983 by david stein (he preferred his name to be all lowercase), one of three members of the New York Gay Male S/M Activists (GMSMA) committee. Standing for 'Safe, Sane and Consensual', it broadly means that the risks of kink activities should be understood by all parties and mitigated where possible ('safe'), that all parties involved should not be under the influence of any kind of substance and should be able to differentiate between fantasy and reality ('sane'), and that all parties have agreed to the activities involved and are free and able to alert other parties if they want to change their mind during play ('consensual').

While some people do still use SSC as an acronym, it's very much a product of the time it was created. BDSM, leathersex and kink were pathologized, and the aim of SSC as language was not only to communicate the GMSMA's values, but also to distance the club from the stereotype of SM and, as stein put it, 'harmful, antisocial, predatory behaviour'. That said, many kinksters – including me – have since criticized it. As I said in *Chapter 3: Sex and Safety*, I don't believe any kind of sex can ever be truly 'safe', only that it can be made 'safer'. I'm also not a fan of the 'sane' in the acronym, as I feel it stigmatizes mental illness and implies that those with mental illnesses cannot engage in BDSM or kink in a healthy way, which is something I don't agree with.

I'm in no way the first person to make these criticisms, and around the turn of the millennium, internet-based BDSM and leatherfolk groups started to come up with alternatives. The most widely used of these new alternatives is RACK, which stands for 'Risk-Aware, Consensual Kink' and was coined by Gary Switch in 1999.

'Risk-aware' within this acronym means that all parties involved in play have a good knowledge of an activity and the risks it carries, and also agree on the steps taken to mitigate it. The meaning of 'consensual' remains the same as in SSC – that all parties involved have agreed to the activities and are free and able to alert other parties if they want to change their mind during play.

INFORMED CONSENT AND RISK

I've already dedicated a whole chapter to sex and safety, including a discussion of some of the risks of sex, so why am I discussing it again here?

Well, kink and BDSM practices carry different risks to 'vanilla' (or non-kinky) practices, and may carry greater risks, in some cases. Kinky play by its nature tends to be 'edgier' than vanilla play and dynamics, and so can cause more intense emotions and responses. And in some cases, playing with kink can skirt the line of legality. In the UK, for example, a person legally cannot consent to injuries that are 'more than merely transient or trifling'. To be able to meaningfully consent to kinky sex or BDSM play, all players must be aware of the risks involved in particular kinds of play and be informed about what steps are being taken to mitigate some of these risks.

Consent is as important in kink and BDSM play as it is in other kinds of sex or sexual play, and it goes beyond having a 'safeword' (although I'll talk more about safewords in the 'Safewords and communication during play' section of this chapter). When we play with kink – especially when newly exploring – we may be playing with situations and emotions that are new to us and to our partners. Our normal ways of checking a partner's state – such as body language, expressions of pain or facial expressions – may not be useful as flags to stop when engaging in kink play. There's a huge diversity of kinds of activities involved in kink and BDSM, and somebody having interest in one doesn't mean they consent to others. And in some forms of play, we voluntarily give up ways in which we can take control of a situation. For example, if we have our wrists bound, we voluntarily give up full use of our hands.

The importance of consent isn't limited to bottoms. Both consent and honesty in consent are mandatory for both tops and bottoms. Sex and sexual experiences are collaborative, and kink and BDSM are no exception.

NEGOTIATION

Negotiation is a key part of kinky sex and incredibly important to informed consent. The form a negotiation takes may vary, depending on what kind of play is involved and who the players are. A couple who have an established vanilla relationship and want to try out some elements of kink will have a different negotiation process to a pair of individuals who've met in a kink community and want to quickly negotiate before play.

Whatever the circumstances, negotiation is an ideal time to establish some important facts. For example:

- What are your desires and fantasies?
- What is your pain tolerance like? What level and kind of pain do you want?
- What are your hard limits (i.e. things that should be entirely avoided)? What about your soft limits (i.e. things that should be approached with caution)?
- Do you have any physical limitations (e.g. muscle or joint issues that might make some movements or positions uncomfortable)?
- How do you want to feel emotionally in a scene/during a session?

- What methods of communication will you use during play?
- Are marks and bruises acceptable? If they are, where and how severe?
- What aftercare needs do you have?

Some people use a checklist for negotiation, where both parties fill out a list of activities with 'yes', 'no' or 'maybe' to indicate their interest in each activity. I think this approach has some usefulness, but is also imperfect and incomplete. Many kinds of play can be used for many different purposes – rope bondage can lend itself to calm, more serene scenes with little or no D/s dynamics, or to D/s-heavy SM scenes.

An alternative approach that I really like is the one used by the educator, author and artist Midori, and discussed in her workshops. While this does start with discussing activities, it goes on to discuss and explore what each party is seeking in terms of feeling. Once this initial period of 'intel gathering' (as Midori puts it) is complete, it's time to use this information to construct and propose a session, and when a proposal has been given, both/all players are able to refine it.

BDSM AND ABUSE

All relationship models can contain abuse, and kinky dynamics and BDSM relationships are no exception. Because of the pathologization of kinky sexualities and the common misconception that BDSM is inherently abusive, a lot of kinksters are reluctant to discuss abusers and abusive relationships within BDSM communities. It's pretty common to hear people claim that 'BDSM isn't abuse, and if it's abuse it's not BDSM', but I don't think this is true or helpful. Abuse does exist within BDSM and kink circles, and playing 'No True Scotsman' with the idea only makes it harder for those within abusive relationships and dynamics to speak about what's happening to them and to seek help.

In *Chapter 1: Desire, Pleasure and Communication*, I discuss some of the warning signs that your relationship may be abusive. These still stand within kinky or BDSM dynamics, but I do want to highlight that it's not just dominants, tops and sadists who can be abusive. Submissives, bottoms and masochists can also be abusive.

SAFEWORDS AND COMMUNICATION DURING PLAY

A lot of 'BDSM 101' style guides talk about the necessity of a safeword – a phrase or word that will immediately stop any scene. While safewords are useful tools, it's worth discussing what they're for in more detail, talking about when they may be less useful, and considering alternatives.

A safeword serves three general purposes:

1. To allow us to relinquish our typical rules of consent for the purpose of fantasy.

2. To allow for a quickly communicated line of exit in emergencies.

3. To allow for unambiguous communication.

Not all dynamics and types of play need a safeword, so long as there is some other method of communication to cover all three points. In some cases, a safeword may not even be the best way to cover all three purposes.

For example, with regards to the first point, not all BDSM play involves playing with typical rules of consent – not even all D/s play does. Even in cases where people are engaging with consent games, taking away all language that normally means 'stop' is not the only way of playing. Specific language can be given away, in that both/all parties are aware it is not to be taken literally – 'stop' or 'please' may mean 'carry on', while other language is to be taken at face value, for example.

For the second point, a safeword may not always be quickly communicated or quickly understood. For dominants, tops and sadists who are deaf or have delays in auditory processing, it can be difficult to understand or interpret safewords quickly. In these cases, other lines of communication – such as asking a bottom to squeeze fingers to indicate they want play to continue, or giving a bottom an object to drop in place of using a safeword – can be more useful. It's also worth considering what the exit strategy is once a safeword has been called. For some kinds of play (e.g. flogging) it's easy to instantly stop, but for others it may take more time. In rope suspension, for example, it takes time to gently lower a bottom to the ground and then more time to take ropes off their body. In some cases, a bottom may call a safeword when they're at their limit for pain, but removing some kinds of gear can actually hurt even more. If somebody calls a safeword when they are at their limit, this may be too late, and a more flexible way of communicating needs and wants during play is potentially both more useful and safer.

And for the third point, a common way to use safewords is the red/yellow/green (or 'traffic light') system. A top or bottom (safewords and other methods of communication during play shouldn't be limited to the bottom) can use 'green' to indicate play can continue or 'red' to communicate that play needs to immediately stop. 'Yellow', however, can have several meanings. For some it means 'slow down', while for others it may mean 'we're approaching my limits, wrap up the scene'. A safeword (or any other line of communication during play, for that matter) is only useful as an unambiguous shortcut if everyone is on the same page with what it means.

This doesn't mean that safewords aren't valuable or useful tools. In many cases they are, which is why they've been so widely adopted. But they're not the only option, and if you have a preference for using plain language that's just as acceptable. Just make sure the communication system you set up with your partner/s allows you to clearly and unambiguously communicate that they should pause the scene and check-in with you or that you want to end the scene.

Playing with the mind

I hope that big block of text didn't scare you off, because now we're going to talk about some of the ways to play with kink. The system I've chosen to divide up this huge topic – discussing playing with the mind and playing with the body separately – is imperfect, but kink and BDSM are so variable and nuanced that any system I use to divide them into sections will be imperfect. I will admit up front that 'playing with the mind' and 'playing with the body' are not discrete categories, and in many contexts the two may intersect with or inform each other. However, this chapter is intended as an introduction to concepts rather than a detailed source of information. If you want a deeper dive into any of these topics, there is some recommended reading in *Further Resources*, at the end of this book.

WHY IS THE MIND IMPORTANT?

As clichéd as it is, the brain is the biggest erogenous zone. Even if we act out play or scenes that are primarily physical – a sadomasochistic scene with no dominance dynamics, as an example – it's our brains that we use to process these actions in terms of what they mean to us. For convenience, I'm using the 'mind'/'brain' as a broad category here, referring to both psychological and emotional sides to kink, as while the two aren't exactly the same, they do overlap.

PLAYING WITH ROLE

The most obvious examples of playing with role involve erotic role-playing – taking on the role of a defined character, be they from popular culture, archetypes or our own imaginations. However, playing with role can also include simply exploring elements or parts of the self that don't always have space to exist within our normal lives. For example, somebody who has a position of authority in their work life may enjoy surrendering this authority within a kink context, as it gives them a chance to explore emotions and parts of themselves that don't always have a presence.

While playing with role is characterized by 'stepping outside' our everyday selves, that doesn't mean that the roles we take on are artificial. In some cases, the roles we want to explore may feel like organic parts of ourselves as much as the roles we play outside a sexual context, like friend, lover, sibling, teacher or student.

There a few different approaches to playing with role, and one may suit your relationship dynamic better than others. You may want to build a scene around defined roles (e.g. Angel/Devil, Morticia/Gomez), around particular acts (e.g. you want an impact scene with some power play, so take on D/s roles) or around wanting to feel a particular way emotionally.

PLAYING WITH POWER

Power play is really common among a wide range of kinky or BDSM dynamics and relationships. Hell, D/s dynamics are based in power play! But power can be played with in less dramatic ways than full D/s dynamics.

Why do people find playing with power interesting? There's a lot of theories, but the take I personally have is that we all navigate dynamics and webs of power in our daily lives. It can be cathartic to express feelings of powerlessness, or find a space to feel powerful in an environment that's controlled and safe. Just as we use fiction to explore scenarios that we wouldn't want to experience in real life, so too can we want to explore roles that involve relinquishing decision-making or feeling in control within sex or play.

Power play can look very different for different people. For some, playing with power goes hand in hand with SM and/or bondage play, while for others D/s dynamics may be the only or primary thing they're interested in. One common distinction between different kinds of playing with power is that of 'high protocol' vs 'low protocol'. While 'protocol' literally just means 'rule', within the context of D/s, I find it helpful to define 'protocol' as being rules about how to carry out certain tasks. Depending on who is playing, this might look like rules about how to address a partner, specific rituals (such as greeting or departing in particular ways) or ongoing tasks.

Playing with the body

While some people may exclusively play with kinky dynamics in a psychological way, physical elements of play often take an important role. For some people, the physical aspects of BDSM play can be their primary interest, with psychological and power play dynamics only important in how they accentuate or complement more physical play.

You may have noticed that the above 'Playing with the mind' section fits neatly into the 'D/s' and 'D' parts of the BDSM acronym (dominance/submission and discipline). In the same way, this section focuses more on the SM and B parts of the acronym (sadism/masochism and bondage). As with the structure of the 'Playing with the mind' section, the sub-categories here aren't mutually exclusive, and do interact with each other.

PAIN AS PLEASURE

One potential aspect of more physical kink play is experiencing pain as pleasure. While not all kink or BDSM does focus on or even include pain, the reasons why some people enjoy feeling pain have been topics of discussion within kink communities for decades.

All the way back in 1987, leather activist Dr Geoff Mains put forward the hypothesis that SM activity stimulates the production of endorphins, and in the years since we've found that to be true. An endorphin is a kind of protein released by the central nervous system. They're actually produced in response to all kinds of pain – think of 'runner's high' or hot massages – and act to block this pain, inducing feelings of euphoria.

If this sounds concerning, I do want to make a very important distinction. 'Pain' and 'harm' are very much different things, and something being painful doesn't necessarily mean that it is harmful. Take eating hot chilis, for example; it may hurt and a person may be averse to eating chilis if it's something they've never done before, but the active ingredient of capsaicin within the chilis is harmless. Over time, a person can learn to dissociate eating chilis with harm, while still fully tasting it.

RESTRAINT

Erotic bondage is, in the broadest possible definition, the restriction of movement. The medium used for this restriction can vary wildly, from rope or devices like cuffs to clothing or just mental restriction.

Bondage can obviously emphasize a power imbalance within play, but can also create feelings of security or other erotic effects on its own. Bondage gear can feel as if it's 'hugging' the body, which can help the bondage bottom feel more relaxed. That's not to say that bondage can't or shouldn't hurt – some people enjoy the feeling of pain that can come with restriction – but it doesn't have to. In many cases, bondage can feel meditative. In others, the restriction of some kinds of movement can concentrate the mind on other types of movement or sensation.

Practical notes

While the bulk of this chapter is theory and discussion, I do want to add a few practical notes towards the end. This isn't a complete guide to carrying out any kind of kink practice, and I would recommend further and more detailed reading.

BONDAGE

A lot of BDSM 101-style content suggests using clothing items you already own – such as scarves or ties – for your first foray into bondage. I would strongly advise against this, especially with silk or slippery materials. While it may save money on gear, material may compact too much, causing the knot to collapse. This can happen with even a small amount of pressure, and once a knot has collapsed it can slip, becoming a lot tighter than expected. The risk of collapsing knots is especially important if you're new to tying knots or still self-teaching.

If you're new to bondage, I'd recommend device bondage, using items like soft handcuffs. While I love rope, I'm also very aware that it's probably the number one way that people get harmed during kink play, and I'd strongly recommend seeking out in-person teaching. If you are playing with rope or bondage tape, it's imperative that you keep safety shears nearby, in case a bottom needs to get out of bondage quickly (e.g. if a fire alarm goes off or if they start to panic).

Always make sure you maintain a way of communication, even if that's non-verbal. For example, if a bottom is tied up and gagged, they can be given an object to drop or a bell to ring if they want or need the top to change something about what they're doing.

Some bondage can hurt. Something hurting doesn't necessarily mean harm has been done, and some people enjoy kinds of bondage that specifically involve pain. However, it's also perfectly fine to only want to engage in bondage that doesn't cause anyone any pain, if that's what you prefer. One thing to note is that if you're new to bondage, it can be difficult to tell the difference between transient pain and pain that indicates harm. Nerve damage from compression is the biggest danger when it comes to bondage, so never tie around joints where nerves are exposed. While some blood flow reduction is inevitable, other kinds of numbness or tingling should be treated as potential cause for alarm. Never leave a bottom alone while they are tied up.

IMPACT PLAY

Impact play is, in the broadest possible sense, hitting somebody for erotic purposes. This can be with parts of the body (e.g. hands) or objects, including both those intended for kink play (e.g. paddles, floggers) or mundane objects with the same effect (e.g. wooden spoons).

If you're new to impact play, using your hands can be an excellent way to ease into it, as the top can feel everything they're doing almost exactly the same way the bottom feels it. When using devices, it's a good idea for tops to try them on themselves first to get an idea of what the sensation feels like – even if they can't hit themselves as hard as the bottom wants to be hit, it's good to know what kind of pain they're going to inflict.

Speaking of types of pain, the broadest distinction is generally thuddy vs stingy pain. 'Thuddy' is generally used to describe firmer impact that happens over a larger area, and generally feels like a punch. 'Stingy' refers to much more concentrated or sharper sensations. Some types of impact gear generally tend to be on the thuddy-stingy spectrum, but even within gear categories there's a lot of variation.

Some of the more common categories of impact implements include paddles, floggers, canes, crops and whips (of which there are many different kinds). These types of toys tend towards different kinds of sensation, and some require more training than others.

Paddles are characterized by their large flat shape, can be made of a variety of materials (including wood, leather etc.) and tend to be more gentle than other impact toys, although this varies depending on the material and shape. They don't require as much training to use as other kinds of impact toys, but it's still important to have a good understanding of the risks of using them.

Floggers sometimes get called whips, but there are some important differences to be aware of. They have a solid rigid handle for easy control, but have an end with many tails (or 'falls' as they're also known), where a whip is normally single-ended. That said, the distinction isn't always clear, as there are some multi-ended whips. It's a bit of a 'I know it when I see it situation', but an important distinction I'd add is that floggers are more about cumulative force than pinpoint accuracy (which is why whips require a lot more training to use safely), and floggers don't require as much physical space. Floggers tend towards being thuddy, but this does vary depending on material – some types of leather have a reputation for being more stingy or thuddy, for example.

Canes tend towards stingy sensation, although this partly

depends on the weight and diameter of the cane, as well as how rigid the material is. Rattan is the most common natural material for canes – although there are other options – with plastic, derlin (which is thuddier and harsher than a lot of other materials) and fibreglass being some of the synthetic options. Canes may be wrapped with a material like leather, which can deepen the sting.

The most well-known style of crop is based on equestrian riding crops – my ex-horse riding tip is that actual riding crops can be utilized for kink, although the handles may not be as padded as riding crops intended for play – but styles that have deviated from this slightly do exist. I'd describe the feeling of crops as a 'stingy thud'.

Regardless of what implement you use for impact play, you should always take safety into account when choosing where to strike. Avoid organs and major bones, and choose areas with more protective fat and muscle. The buttocks or upper thighs are good places to start experimenting with impact play. Always remember to have solid communication methods established before you play, and to establish a barometer of the bottom's pain tolerances. This isn't just a question of hardness, but also types of play, as some people have different tolerances for thuddy vs stingy impact (although generally people have higher tolerances for thuddy). As a top, it's worth noting that bruising and redness aren't consistent and can happen in all kinds of ways, so while you shouldn't ignore them, on their own they are not a good indicator of how hard you're hitting somebody.

Further reading

As I said earlier, this chapter doesn't and can't give you a full insight into kink and BDSM. There's enough variety and diversity in kink practices that it could fill an entire library, let alone a book! I'm aware that very little of this chapter is centred on practical tips, and this is on purpose. I believe that in-person lessons are one of the best ways to learn BDSM techniques safely, and I encourage you to reach out to your local kink, leather or BDSM communities to see if there are workshops or other kinds of teaching available to you. However, I'm aware that not everyone has these communities available to them, and that even where these communities do exist they may be hostile to trans people, LGBQ people, or people of colour. While my book suggestions in *Further Resources* can't replace in-person learning, they can still be a valuable next step.

I do want to add a disclaimer that a lot of the books in the *Further Resources* list were written in the 1990s or 2000s, and the language they use (especially around gender and sexuality) can be outdated. However, they still have valuable things to say, so I still want to recommend them, even if it's with a caveat.

One last thing

You've made it to the end of this book! We've covered a lot of ground, so if you're still unsure about, challenged by or still working out your feelings on any of the topics or information we've covered, take some time to re-read a section, or step away from this book for a little while to think things over. Learning about sex is a process that takes up our whole lives, so if you aren't ready for any topics, you might be later, and even if you are ready right now, you may want to re-approach some of the topics at a later date.

While I've tried to cover topics with a reasonable amount of depth, the topic of trans-centred sex education is so broad that I had to omit some information, so if you'd like to do some extra reading, there's a *Further Resources* section after this, with everything organized by chapter relevance.

I hope – if you are a trans person reading this book – that you've found some tools within it to help empower yourself when it comes to your sexuality, just as I found it an empowering experience to research and write it. And if you are a cisgender person reading it, I hope it has been useful for and empowering to you too, whether that be applying some of the information to your own sex life, using it to inform your relationship with a transgender partner, or simply being more aware of sexual experiences that are not your own.

Further Resources

GENERAL
- ♥ Allison Moon, *Girl Sex 101* (2014)
- ♥ Zoë Ligon, *Carnal Knowledge: Sex Education You Didn't Get in School* (2020)
- ♥ Ruby Rare, *Sex Ed: A Guide for Adults* (2020)

DESIRE, PLEASURE AND COMMUNICATION
- ♥ Emily Nagoski, *Come As You Are: The Surprising New Science That Will Transform Your Sex Life* (2015)

ANATOMY AND BODIES
- ♥ Finlay Games, *Top to Bottom: A Memoir and Personal Guide Through Phalloplasty* (2021)

SEX AND SAFETY
- ♥ Brook.org.uk

MANUAL SEX AND GRINDING
- ♥ Mira Bellwether, *Fucking Trans Women #0* (2013)

ANAL SEX

- ♥ Carlyle Jansen, *Anal Sex Basics: The Beginner's Guide to Maximizing Anal Pleasure for Every Body* (2016)

KINK

GENERAL

- ♥ Dossie Easton and Janet W. Hardy, *The New Topping Book* (2002)
- ♥ Dossie Easton and Janet W. Hardy, *The New Bottoming Book* (2001)

ROLE-PLAY

- ♥ Deborah Addington, *Fantasy Made Flesh: The Essential Guide to Erotic Roleplay* (2003)

BONDAGE

- ♥ Mistress Couple, *The Ultimate Guide to Bondage: Creating Intimacy Through the Art of Restraint* (2020)
- ♥ Lee Harrington, *Shibari You Can Use: Japanese Rope Bondage and Erotic Macramé* (2015)
- ♥ Evie Vane, *Better Bondage for Every Body* (2017)

IMPACT PLAY

- ♥ Lady Green, *The Compleat Spanker* (1996)
- ♥ Joseph W. Bean, *Flogging* (2000)

OTHER

- ♥ Cory Silverberg and Miriam Kaufman, *Ultimate Guide to Sex and Disability: For All of Us Who Live with Disabilities, Chronic Pain & Illness* (2003)
- ♥ A. Andrews, *A Quick & Easy Guide to Sex & Disability* (2020)

Endnotes

1   James, S.E., Herman, J., Keisling, M., Mottet, L. & Ma'ayan, A. (2019) 2015 U.S. Transgender Survey (USTS). Inter-university Consortium for Political and Social Research [distributor], 22 May. https://doi.org/10.3886/ICPSR37229.v1.

2   Hembree, W.C., Cohen-Kettenis, P., Delemarre-Van De Waal, H.A., Gooren, L.J. et al. (2009) 'Endocrine treatment of transsexual persons: An Endocrine Society clinical practice guideline.' *The Journal of Clinical Endocrinology & Metabolism*, 94(9), 3132–3154.

3   Seal, L.J. (2017) 'Hormone Treatment for Transgender Adults.' In W.P. Bouman & J. Arcelus (eds), *The Transgender Handbook: A Guide for Transgender People, Their Families and Professionals* (pp.227–249). New York, NY: Nova Science Publishers.

4   Kent, M.K., Winoker, J.S. & Grotas, A.B. (2018) 'Effects of feminizing hormones on sperm production and malignant changes: Microscopic examination of post orchiectomy specimens in transwomen.' *Urology*, 121, 9–96.

5   Birse, K.D., Kratzer, K., Zuend, C.F., Mutch, S. et al. (2020) 'The neovaginal microbiome of transgender women post-gender reassignment surgery.' *Microbiome*, 8, 61. https://doi.org/10.1186/s40168-020-00804-1.

6   Frey, J.D., Poudrier, G., Chiodo, M.V. & Hazen, A. (2016) 'A systematic review of metoidioplasty and radial forearm flap phalloplasty in female-to-male transgender genital reconstruction: Is the "ideal" neophallus an achievable goal?' *Plastic and Reconstructive Surgery – Global Open: December 2016*, 4(12), e1131. doi: 10.1097/GOX.0000000000001131.

7   Lindberg, L.D., Maddow-Zimnet, I. & Boonstra, H. (2016) 'Changes in adolescents' receipt of sex education, 2006–2013.' *Journal of Adolescent Health*, 58(6), 621–627.

8   James, C., Harfouche, M., Welton, N., Turner, K. et al. (2020) 'Herpes simplex

virus: Global infection prevalence and incidence estimates, 2016.' *Bulletin of the World Health Organization*, 98, 315–329. doi: 10.2471/BLT.19.237149.

9   Radix, A.E., Harris, A.B., Belkind, U., Ting, J. & Goldstein, Z.G. (2019) 'Chlamydia trachomatis infection of the neovagina in transgender women.' *Open Forum Infectious Diseases*, 6(11). doi: 10.1093/ofid/ofz470.

10   Grant, R., Lama, J., Anderson, P., McMahan, V. *et al.* (2010). 'Preexposure chemoprophylaxis for HIV prevention in men who have sex with men.' *New England Journal of Medicine*, 363, 2587–2599. doi: 10.1056/NEJMoa1011205.

11   Antebi-Gruszka, N., Talen, A.J., Reisner, S.L. & Rendina, H.J. (2020) 'Sociodemographic and behavioural factors associated with testing for HIV and STIs in a US nationwide sample of transgender men who have sex with men.' *Sexually Transmitted Infections*, 96(6), 422–427.

12   Pasquino, A.M., Pucarelli, I., Accardo, F., Demiraj, V., Segni, M. & Di Nardo, R. (2008) 'Long-term observation of 87 girls with idiopathic central precocious puberty treated with gonadotropin-releasing hormone analogs: Impact on adult height, body mass index, bone mineral content, and reproductive function.' *Journal of Clinical Endocrinology & Metabolism*, 93(1), 190–195.

13   Light, A., Obedin-Maliver, J., Sevelius, J. & Kerns, J. (2014) 'Transgender men who experienced pregnancy after female-to-male gender transitioning.' *Obstetrics & Gynecology*, 124(6), 1120–1127. doi: 10.1097/AOG.0000000000000540.

14   Moseson, H., Fix, L., Ragosta, S., Forsberg, H. *et al.* (2020) 'Abortion experiences and preferences of transgender, nonbinary, and gender-expansive people in the United States.' *American Journal of Obstetrics & Gynecology*, 224(4), 376-E1–376-E11.

15   Moseson, H., Fix, L., Ragosta, S., Forsberg, H. *et al.* (2020) 'Abortion experiences and preferences of transgender, nonbinary, and gender-expansive people in the United States.' *American Journal of Obstetrics & Gynecology*, 224(4), 376-E1–376-E11.

16   Stonewall (2017) *LGBT in Britain – Trans Report* [online]. Available at: www.stonewall.org.uk/lgbt-britain-trans-report.

17   Anderson, T.A., Schick, V., Herbenick, D., Dodge, B. & Fortenberry, J.D. (2014) 'A study of human papillomavirus on vaginally inserted sex toys, before and after cleaning, among women who have sex with women and men.' *Sexually Transmitted Infections* 2014, 90(7), 529–531.

18   Brown, J.M., Hess, K.L., Brown, S., Murphy, C., Waldman, A.L. & Hezareh, M. (2013) 'Intravaginal practices and risk of bacterial vaginosis and candidiasis infection among a cohort of women in the United States.' *Obstetrics & Gynecology*, 121(4), 773–780. doi: 10.1097/AOG.0b013e31828786f8.

19 Schreiber, C.A., Meyn, L.A., Creinin, M.D., Barnhart, K.T. & Hillier, S.L. (2006) 'Effects of long-term use of nonoxynol-9 on vaginal flora.' *Obstetrics and Gynecology*, 107(1), 136–143. doi: 10.1097/01.AOG.0000189094.21099.4a.

20 Stockdale, C.K. & Lawson, H.W. (2014) '2013 Vulvodynia Guideline update.' *Journal of Lower Genital Tract Disease*, 18(2), 93–100. doi: 10.1097/LGT.0000000000000021.

21 Hancock, E. (2014) *A Primer on Touch*. Baltimore, MD: Johns Hopkins University.

22 Herbenick, D., Fu, J., Arter, J., Sanders, S.A. & Dodge, B. (2018) 'Women's experiences with genital touching, sexual pleasure, and orgasm: Results from a U.S. probability sample of women ages 18 to 94.' *Journal of Sex & Marital Therapy*, 44(2), 201–212. doi: 10.1080/0092623X.2017.1346530.

Index